Contents

Introduction

The Shadow Man of Accrington

Boon Kirk Farm   19 – 25

The Darwen School Apparitions   26 – 40

A Fond Farewell?   41 - 42

A Clayton-le-Moors Haunting and Pit Disaster   43 – 54

Wood Terrace   55 – 60

Curry Electrical Shop, Oldham   61 – 68

The Little Boy With No Legs   69 – 73

Did my Father See Ghosts?   74 – 78

Pendle Hill   79 – 102

Proof of an Afterlife?   103 – 106

Unit Four Cinema, Accrington   107 – 112

The Fisherman's Cottage   113 – 119

Haunted Hospitals   120 – 127

The Strange Story of Huntroyd Hall   128 – 131

Boggarts and More Boggarts   132 – 137

Ley Lines   138 – 144

Short Stories   145 – 156

Famously Haunted Lancashire   157 - 167

Introduction

People are fascinated by ghost stories and the unexplained. Over recent years there has been a noticeable increase in television programmes and social media channels where ghost 'hunters' spend the night in a haunted location, usually in pitch black darkness, with shaky hand held cameras, shouting and screaming at every little noise. Most of these programmes don't seem to show any definitive evidence of ghosts, although I'm sure that there is *some* activity you could attribute to the paranormal. Being locked away in a dungeon, or in a 'haunted' room, all by yourself with your senses already heightened to the smallest sound or movement certainly makes for a frightened and tense presenter, and great television entertainment. I can say, however, from personal experience that if you do a see a ghost then often your reaction is somewhat different to hysterical screams and a shaky hand held camera.

So, putting entertainment purposes aside for a moment, do people really see ghosts? Well, there are any number of reports of ghosts from all over the world, both malevolent and benign, and many books on the subject. In Lancashire, for instance, there are dozens of haunted houses and great Halls. Salmesbury Hall near Preston is world famous for its White Lady. Turton Tower near Bolton is renowned for its pair of human skulls which reportedly 'scream' and cause all manner of activity if removed from a niche in the wall which they currently. Indeed, there are many books on the subject of haunted houses and ghosts from every region of the United

Kingdom, and indeed the world. When I decided to write this book, it was not only because I have personally seen some strange things over the years, many of which I would say were 'paranormal' experiences, but talking to friends, family and acquaintances, I have found that I am not alone and I have been amazed at the number of people who were quite willing to tell me their own spooky stories. As well as ghosts there are some references to Unidentified Flying Objects (or UFO's), as well as a brief history of Lancashire, its countryside, people and strange energies and how everything is connected in a way that we really do not understand!

Ghosts come in many different types of manifestations. But why do people see ghosts? I believe the theory that a paranormal event is an energy or 'frequency' that is attached to a specific place or location. Perhaps some people are more attuned to that 'frequency' than others, and that is why they 'see' ghosts. I have been to many 'haunted' locations over the years, some of them the famous ones I have mentioned, and not once have I seen White Lady or heard a skull screaming. A good analogy is tuning an old radio dial into a station. To get a precise signal you have to finely tune the dial, otherwise all you get is static. Think of people who can see ghosts or witness paranormal events as being 'fine tuned'.

As you read through the stories in this book you will understand that on a personal level, it is not always a vision of something paranormal, it is often just a feeling such as unease, upset, depression or unexplainable fear. Often objects are moved or thrown, and some of the kind people who have allowed me to use their stories in this book have reported physical sensations as well as strange occurrences and visions. I really wanted this book to be about not only my personal experiences but those of others as well. These are very personal stories that would otherwise remain untold.

The Different Types of Ghost

Manifestations or hauntings often fall into a particular category of ghost. In this book I try to describe some of the experiences I have had, and try to explain how they could have happened. The stories I have gathered during my research are fascinating, and every one included in this book I felt were credible. Whilst some may say they are easy to explain, I leave it to the reader to make up their own mind.

Recordings of Past Events

Some people believe that certain events over time are somehow recorded, and replayed at certain other times in the future. The theory is that some traumatic or highly emotional event happened in a particular place and that somehow it has been 'recorded' into the very space that it took place in. This could be the fabric of the building, the ground on which it happened or just the 'space' in which the event took place. What triggers these replays in unknown, indeed the very theory itself holds no basis in science at all. These types of recordings are very common, the White lady of Salmesbury Hall is often seen traversing the road near to the hall, causing the occasional panic in motorists who see the filmy shape of a woman too late and drive straight through it. When I was shown round a school in Darwen in East Lancashire I was told about the spirit of a woman who seemed to be in mourning, and followed the same path each time (my theory on this is in that particular chapter). These manifestations don't interact with anyone or anything around them, and pass through walls or objects as if they were not there. Sometimes, if the fabric of the building has been altered, say for instance the floor has been raised, and then often these types of ghosts can be seen to have part of their body lower than the new floor level, cut off at the knee for instance, following the original floor.

Presences

Many people do not see a conventional ghost or hear traditional footsteps walking down an empty corridor, but rather they sense a presence which they can't explain. Perhaps in these cases the 'tuning' is slightly off, or perhaps the energy simply isn't strong enough to visually or audibly manifest itself. People who are sensitive to whatever energy is released often report the same feelings as others, without prior knowledge. People can sense malevolent or disturbing energy, whilst others occasionally feel some are benign, even friendly.

Poltergeists

The word 'Poltergeist' is German for 'Noisy Ghost' which, given the behaviour of many Poltergeists, is rather apt. Not only are they noisy, in that they make banging and crashing noises, but they also move objects, often throwing them around. Poltergeists tend to focus on one person, usually a teenage child. There is no rational explanation for this, but maybe the person most affected is themselves somehow creating the energy or focusing energy around them. Teenagers tend to be highly emotional, and this maybe an insight in to what causes these types of haunting. Perhaps their highly charged emotional energy is somehow manifesting itself in a kinetic force, one that can create noises and move objects. Perhaps their highly emotional state may act as an 'anchor' to our world or a gateway for malevolent spirits to come through to our plane of existence. Whatever the cause, Poltergeists are both fascinating and terrifying and remain the archetypal behaviour of a ghost for most people interested in the paranormal.

Interactive ghosts

During my research I have found many examples of what I would describe as an 'Interactive Ghost'. These are ghosts who react to the people and surroundings around them and rarely show the mischievousness or malevolence of Poltergeists. Interactive Ghosts seems aware of our presence and may react to questions or requests. Some people believe these types of ghosts are proof positive of an afterlife, especially where they identify themselves as someone who has died, and can offer up information only that dead person would know. Often these are family members or benign spirits somehow attached to a place or building.

Time Slips

It is possible that ghosts are in fact 'Time Slips'. This is where a window opens up between two times, allowing people on either side of the window to see and even interact with each other. Whether one or both actually moves in time cannot be determined with any certainty, although reported incidents of people encountering time slips would seem to suggest they actually do. One of the most reported places this happens is Bold Street in Liverpool, where people have reported being transported to another time entirely, and interacting with their surroundings, even walking around from their original location. To the people of that time, it is entirely possible that an interloper would manifest him or herself as a 'ghost'. This opens up the intriguing possibility that time slips could physically move someone both forward and backwards in time. For instance, one gentleman reported walking out of a shop onto Bold Street only to suddenly find himself surrounded by what he perceived as a Victorian scene, and to him it seemed very real indeed. Perhaps, conversely, reports of past instances intruding into our time frame and appearing as ghosts would seem very real to the people in the past suddenly catapulted into the future. There are numerous reports from all over the United Kingdom of 'phantom armies' of Roman soldiers suddenly appearing, or medieval soldiers reappearing at the sight of famous battles, Bosworth Field being a good example. Indeed, there is a recently discovered Roman Road not too far from where I live, which leads to the Roman town of Ribchester on the navigable part of the River Ribble. Local legend tells of ghostly footsteps and the clanking of armour and glimpses of Roman legionaries marching through the woods along the old road. Perhaps this is an example of a time slip, and who knows what the soldiers of the past would make if they suddenly came face to face with someone from the 21st Century!

The Shadow Man of the Accrington Conservative Club

Source – Author

When – 1980's

A strange shadowy figure, demonic presences, poltergeist activity and flying glassware, the Accrington Conservative Club had them in abundance! Stone built in the gothic style it was steeped in history. There were hidden dusty rooms creaking with dark menace and a Victorian staircase that hinted of something terrifying around the corner. Who, or what, haunted this building and why? Did I witness a poltergeist smashing a glass on the floor? Did I see a 'Shadow Man' looming over the bar ?

Built in 1890, this magnificent Grade II listed building is currently in a dire state of disrepair. Situated on Cannon Street in Accrington town centre, the building was briefly a nightclub until 2003 when a patron tragically died outside the premises. Prior to this, the Conservative Club regularly held dances on its magnificent 3rd floor ballroom, one of only two sprung dance floors (the other being the Tower Ballroom in Blackpool) and regular private parties on its two 2nd floor bars and function rooms. The ground floor bar was members only, with two full size snooker tables built by the Riley Snooker and Billiard Table Company. There was dusty old red velvet seating and dark wood panelling that oozed history. The building felt dark though, oppressive and uncomfortable at times with an atmosphere all of its own. Following the demise of the nightclub, aptly named 'Churchills', the building was closed and has suffered from vandalism and a fire which gutted the premises.

The derelict building, shortly before the fire.

As I write this in early 2019, I read in the local press that Town Planners have approved an application to convert the building into private flats.

The Conservative Club was the largest of its kind in the country, and was built by WJ Morely and G Woodhouse, funded by Mr Howard, who was a partner with Mr Bullough in one of the largest textile machinery factories in Britain. I was told by a former Steward of the club, Bernard, that the Cannon Street Baptist Church, directly across the road was built as a statement of sobriety and worship to countermand the Club and it is less than sober patrons, and that a competition ensued as to which building could be completed the tallest. I believe that the Club won, by a good foot! Sadly, it would seem that the church has also fallen in to disrepair and is also earmarked to be converted into flats.

My association with the Conservative Club goes back years. My father was a member of the Committee for many years and held the position of Treasurer. At the time, in the late 1970's and 1980's the Club was, I believe, bankrolled by Thwaites Brewery of Blackburn, and held regular Saturday night dances in the Ballroom, to which people came from miles around. When I started working there in the late 1980's as a glass collector whilst studying at College, the stuffy old time atmosphere of the Ballroom with its 'Big Bands' and ageing clientele were like something from the 1950's. Flares and quiff's were the order of the day and the smell of Brylcreem still lingers with me today. If I said the average age of the patrons was in their 50's and 60's even then it wouldn't be an understatement. The ballroom was magnificent though. It had a high ceiling with large stained-glass windows along either side. At one end was the bar and at the other, the stage. There was a presence that felt uncomfortable and many staff refused to go through the back to check the fire escape door. As I turned 18, I graduated to serving behind the bar and occasionally worked on the ground floor as well as stocking the bars on weekend mornings. I also played snooker on a weekday evenings, and characters such as Alex 'Hurricane' Higgins occasionally frequented the Club and played a few games on the green baize. My father, who played in the Lancashire Amateur Snooker Competitions, was adamant he had played 'The Hurricane' in a friendly match at the Club one evening and beaten him.

When I first started working at the Club I remember having a pep talk from Bernard - how to pull a pint with a proper 'head', not to give short measures because it upset the members, who to look out for as potential trouble makers after a few too many Barley Wines….. that sort of thing. On one particular quiet midweek evening I was manning the members bar on my own, and thoroughly bored. The bar itself was fairly long and straight, maybe about 25 foot or so from memory with an opening to my left into the snooker room. It was made of dark wood, perhaps stained oak, and was lacquered. It added to the already dark atmosphere of the room. There was nobody playing snooker that evening and I recall not many people had been in for a drink. Bernard was pottering about on the upstairs floors leaving me alone for most of the evening. As I was stood with my back against the rear of the bar, the opening to the snooker room to my left, I saw a figure out of the corner of my eye. As I turned my head to see who it was, (I presumed a customer had somehow slipped past my gaze and gone into the adjoining room), I saw the outline of a tall man, dressed in long dark clothes with what looked like an angular hat, rather like a Fedora, leaning on the bar. It had no facial features at all. The figure was opaque, like a thick mist, and quite substantial. It had no arms that I could see, and because it was behind a waist high bar I could not see its legs. It was leaning over towards me, seemingly looking for something down on the floor or behind the bar. The figure was tall and thin, much thinner than a real person and looked 'stretched' out almost as if it was being pulled from both ends! All this was indelibly etched into my memory, despite the figure slowly fading to a mist and disappearing after only a few seconds. At first I felt amazement, but then suddenly my heart started to beat faster as I panicked and realised what I had seen. I had actually seen a ghost!

No sooner than the figure had faded away than I rang the upstairs bars on the internal phone until Bernard answered and came down. He could tell I was somewhat disturbed as I blurted out something about a ghost. In a fairly calm manner he explained that there was indeed a ghost that occasionally manifested itself at the end of the bar. Quite a few members of staff, himself included, had seen him. Although quite a few people had seen this apparition, nobody knew who he was. They all described it as tall and shadowy, and when I told Bernard it looked 'stretched', he nodded and agreed. He had seen that too. I would have liked to have seen the figure again, as, in truth, I didn't feel any malevolence coming from it, but despite working in the ground floor bar many times, and often locking up at the end of the night when I was on my own , I only saw that apparition that one time.

I believe the ghost may have been a recording type of manifestation rather than an apparition that was aware of me and my surroundings. It did not interact with me, or with others who said they had seen it too and I cannot say whether it was conscious or aware I was present in the same space. I did not feel it was threatening; it was simply momentarily there. Was this an example of phenomena that is now recognised as a 'Shadow Man'? Many religions and beliefs describe shadowy spiritual beings or supernatural entities such as 'shades' or shadowy creatures and have long been a staple of folklore and ghost stories. Perhaps my encounter was indeed with one of these shadowy figures. The term 'Shadow Person' was not popularised in modern paranormal circles until the early 2000's, thanks mainly to late night American radio paranormal broadcasts such as 'Coast 2 Coast AM' hosted by the late Art Bell. When I had this encounter, the term and phenomena had been long forgotten.

Other parts of the club were haunted too. The cellar had a dark presence and a foreboding atmosphere. I often felt uneasy going down the stairs on my own to change barrels or bring crates of bottles up to restock the bar. It was dimly lit, with a low ceiling and a constant damp, musty smell. It felt wholly unwelcoming! There was an ingenious 'dumb waiter' lift that ran up to all three floors so that heavy crates could be loaded and sent up to where they were needed (I do recall some fellow members of staff who went up and down in it as a joke – the horseplay and foolishness of youth !). One incident which stands out was when I was asked to whitewash the cellar walls for some extra holiday spending money.

One week I spent a few hours a day down there whitewashing the cellar walls. In truth I was uneasy as I didn't like the atmosphere and the claustrophobic nature of the low stone ceilings and cold stone floor and walls. I would leave in the afternoon feeling chilled to the bone. There had been an occasional bang or strange noise which I put down to pipes settling, or gas in the barrels, and got on with the task at hand. On the final morning, however, I went down early and felt more uneasy than normal. Despite it being early summer and fairly warm outside, it felt absolutely freezing in the cellar that morning, and so cold that I recall seeing my breath condensing as I breathed out. This was most definitely out of the ordinary and disturbing. As I descended the stairs I was aware of something oppressive and unpleasant and for a split second I saw a figure standing at the far end of the cellar against the wall. The hairs on the back of my neck stood up, and stayed up, as I tried to focus on what it was. The cellar lights were on, but they were quite dim and didn't really illuminate the whole of the cellar, particularly the far wall. To this day, I am convinced there was something evil in the cellar that morning and that it was thoroughly unpleasant. The sudden drop in temperature would seem to suggest classic paranormal activity. The figure was, as with the ghost in the bar upstairs, very tall but seemed to stoop almost to avoid touching the low ceiling. I'm 6ft 2" tall and the ceiling just cleared my head, so whatever this was, it was taller than I. I remember for a few seconds it looked at me, almost leering. I thought I could make out facial features, perhaps a beard and straggly unkempt hair, and it was dressed in some sort of workman's outfit, wearing a heavy coat with a cap. Unlike the apparition in the ground floor bar area, this was most definitely aware of my presence and altogether more unpleasant and sinister. It was also easier to make out, was less shadowy and much more of a clear apparition. I breathed a sigh of relief when it suddenly disappeared, as quickly as it had appeared and I hurriedly went back upstairs feeling shaken and very afraid. By this time, Bernard had retired, and the new Steward, John, wasn't convinced that there was a ghost in his cellar and shrugged off my story as little more than fantasy, which annoyed me somewhat. He must have seen that I was visibly shaken and I refused to finish the last bit of wall. I took payment for what I had done and vowed never to go back down to the cellar on my own. Unlike the ground floor ghost, this felt altogether different and certainly more threatening. I felt it was fully aware of my presence and felt hugely uneasy when it looked directly at me. This entity, whatever it was, was definitely 'there' of 'of that moment in time' and was malevolent and threatening. Who was this character and why was he so attached to the cellar? Whoever he was, at that moment, he did not want me in his space.

The third incident of paranormal activity I witnessed at the club again happened in daylight, and was a Saturday morning whilst I was up in the ballroom stocking the bar. There was only myself and John in the building, and he was busy stocking the ground floor bar and changing barrels in the cellar. John was adamant he never saw anything in the cellar and was somewhat annoyed when I often refused to go down on my own.

The derelict ballroom, facing towards the bar.

I had loaded the Dumb Waiter with crates of bottles and after sending the lift on its way, trudged up the three flights of winding stairs to the ballroom. I used to reach the top and lean over the dark wooden balustrade, looking down the centre of the staircase to the ground floor below. There was something that made me keep doing it; perhaps some unknown force was trying to make contact. Whatever the reason, something drew me to that staircase time and time again. On this occasion I went into the storeroom and was unloading the crates when I suddenly heard glass smashing in the bar. It was loud and made me jump and I hurried through to see if anyone else was there. There was no one. I was alone. Suddenly I felt uneasy. Looking down I saw glass strewn across the floor behind the bar. How had this happened I wondered? From the pieces of glass, I realised it was a barrel handled pint glass. These types of glasses are rare now, but imagine a heavy, thick round glass with dimpled sides and a handle. They were popular back in the day with working men who demanded 'a proper pint of bitter in a real pint glass with a handle'. These glasses were kept above the bar hanging on very sturdy hooks, very deeply curved so as to make sure the glasses didn't fall off. In order to get a glass off the hook you had to lift it upwards and sideways and because of its weight and shape there was absolutely no way it could simply slip or fall off. All the glasses were hanging there apart from one empty hook. I was astonished. I stood and looked at the shattered glass trying to work out how it could have fallen on the floor with such force without being physically lifted off. There was no one else around, and there was no way someone could have got through into the bar, smashed the glass and exited the same way as I was coming in to the bar a couple of seconds after hearing the noise. My only conclusion was that someone, or something, had physically lifted the glass off the hook and thrown it on the floor. At this point I started to feel something disturbing, like an actual physical threat. I felt like there was something there that didn't like me. Whether this was a reaction to a very clear example of paranormal activity, or a change in the atmosphere that I was sensing, is difficult to say. What I do question is if this was a natural occurrence, for example, the glass simply fell off the hook, why did it happen at that particular time? To my knowledge nobody in the club had ever mentioned witnessing a similar incident themselves. Why did the glass fall off a substantial hook, which was still screwed into the ceiling of the bar, and undamaged, at the very moment I was in the stockroom alone, in broad daylight? If there were, for instance vibrations that caused it to fall, how did it lift up half an inch so that the handle could clear the hook, and why just this one glass? Why not others? Even after all these years I am convinced that the glass was deliberately removed from the hook and thrown on the floor by an unseen paranormal force in order to frighten me.

It was not long afterwards that I finished working at the club. I mentioned my experiences in passing to a few people who frequented the Conservative Club and although nobody admitted seeing or feeling anything out of the ordinary, the looks and nods some gave me, including those of my own father when I later told him, led me to believe that I wasn't the only one who had witnessed some strange occurrences in the Club.

Old buildings like the Accrington Conservative Club have seen years of history and in my opinion it is not surprising they hold echoes of their past within their structure and foundations. There was a dark, unwelcoming atmosphere in parts of the building. The old dusty furnishings and air of neglect only added to the atmosphere. Although my time spent there was over 30 years ago, these incidents have remained with me as if they happened yesterday. I remain convinced that there were at least two ghosts or entities in the building, and I would not be surprised if there were more, and I witnessed an incident that can only be described as poltergeist activity. Whether the malevolent cellar ghost roamed around the building and was responsible for the smashed pint glass on the third floor I do not know, but it would be interesting to see if there are any further manifestations when the building is finally renovated.

Boon Kirk Farm

Source – Family Member

When – 1990's

Heavy nocturnal footsteps, a floating whisky glass and a hidden secret room – Boon Kirk Farm was steeped in history and paranormal activity. Family members still talk about their frightening experiences. This was a very old haunted farmhouse!

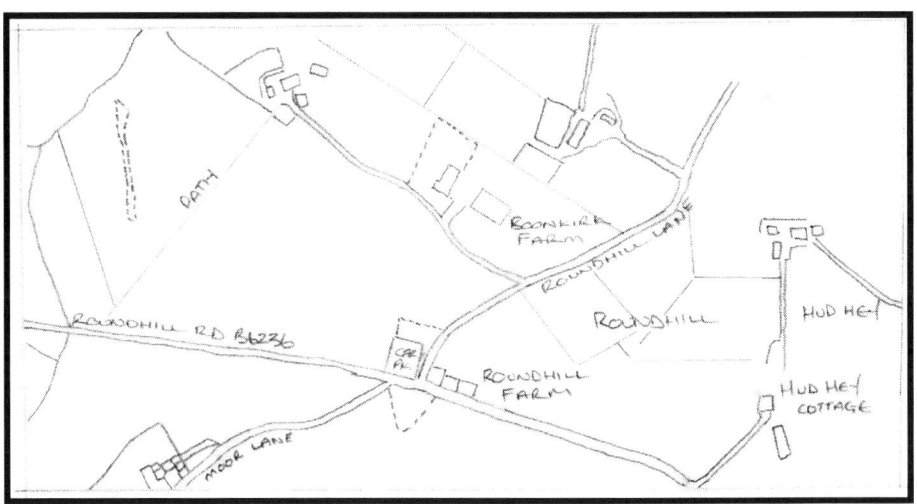

Map of location of Boon Kirk Farm © Craig Bryant

Dating back to the 16th century, Boon Kirk Farm is situated near to Rising Bridge, a small village between Haslingden and Accrington. It is in a rather exposed position, high on the moors close to the Farmer's Glory Pub (now a rather good Indian restaurant), overlooking the village and beyond to the south and the urban conurbations of Bury and Manchester. It is open to the harsh Lancashire weather on three sides, with a planting of trees along the western end to deflect the worst of the winter weather. It can be foreboding and unforgiving when the weather turns, with harsh westerly storms that batter the moorland high about the industrial towns and villages of East Lancashire. The moors are sparse and boggy with no trees and short stubbly grasses and ferns that hold in the water. It is not a place you want to be caught out in the open when a storm hits!

Boon Kirk Farm sits on these unforgiving moors, often taking the worst of the weather. It was cold and draughty and the only heating was provided by wood burning stoves and a Range in the kitchen. The doors and windows would whistle to the tune of the storm outside, and doors would open and bang shut, seemingly by some unknown hand. The dark, brooding Lancashire skies weigh heavily on the moors surrounding Boon Kirk, and on the farm itself.

The farm was one of two cottages attached to a barn, and is reputedly one of the oldest surviving documented buildings in Lancashire. It was part of the Duke of Buccleuch's Estate who, interestingly, still holds the mineral rights on the land. It is believed one of the Dukes land agents in times gone by was Scottish, thus the rather Celtic name attached to a farm in Lancashire!

The Farm land is sparse and boggy, and the few good fields are south facing. They get the best sun in summer, but still bear the brunt of autumn and winter storms. An elderly lady who lived in one of the cottages at the turn of the 20th Century, before it was converted into one dwelling, remembered the toilets being a wooden shack at the end of the field and there was an old tin bath, used for bathing, around the back of the house that the horses used to drink from. She remembered the cold, stone floor, and that you had to step down from the kitchen into the front room and then back up again into the second room. Her most vivid memory was slamming a door and cutting a rat in two!

There are census records that may give a clue to who is still haunting Boon Kirk Farm. Benjamin Howarth and Mary Catlow lived in the farm in the 1820's and records show a daughter, Alice, born in 1820.

In 1851 there were 27 people living in the two cottages, most were factory workers in the booming textile industry. Following the death of the owner of the local factories (he did not leave any sons to take over the family business), this dwindled to 9.

Another record shows the marriage of 25-year-old John Albert Pollard of Boon Kirk Farm to 22-year-old Tabitha Knowles of Baxenden. The Groom's Father was Henry Pollard who was a deceased 'Cloth Looker', also from Boon Kirk.

When Sarah's family moved in it was no longer a working farm. They had a dog kennel and cattery business as well as a number of household pets. The dogs, and Miffy the Doberman especially, would stare into space as if looking at something only they could see. The upkeep of such an old farm was a year-round endeavour and

Sarah recalls her grandfather and stepfather spending most of their time painting and repairing the house from the battering the Lancashire weather gave it. Although it had wooden floors upstairs, they discovered these were laid across the original stone flagging and the downstairs floor was mainly stone flags, with a deep cellar below. The walls were stone built to survive the harshest weather, and were two or three feet thick. There was a cellar, but this had been filled in and was no longer accessible. Interestingly, a few hundred years ago it wasn't uncommon to bury the dead in the cellar of properties such as Boon Kirk Farm. Often the winters were so cold that the ground was either too boggy or too frozen to dig a grave, and coupled with the isolation of many farms, it was easier to deal with a dead body in that way rather than leave it for what could amount to weeks before being able to move it to a church or graveyard. I have been told that there is a 'Coffin Road' – an old track that leads over Pendle Hill which was used to transport the dead to a more fitting resting place from the many isolated farmsteads that dotted the slopes of this famous hill, but only if the relatives had the money to pay for such a journey. Because of the remoteness of Boon Kirk, it is entirely possible that there was at least one body buried in the cellar. Why the cellar had been filled in was a mystery – perhaps it was to keep something down there!

Even in the 1990's there was no mains water only a natural water spring and no mains gas. There was, thankfully, mains electricity although this could become unreliable as you will read later! It was cold, it was draughty and it was damp and the constant upkeep, both in time and cost, was what eventually persuaded Sarah's family to sell the farm. Whenever we are in the area we drive past, remarking on its dark brooding silhouette against an often leaden and grey Lancashire sky as we approach down the country lane that runs parallel with the farm.

Sarah's family shared Boon Kirk Farm with at least one ghost. The activity was typical of that of a poltergeist. It was known to throw objects and open and close doors at will. There were a number of strange incidents including objects disappearing and appearing in totally different places, heavy footfalls and door slamming. The activity intensified after my mother-in-law decided to sell the farm, and invited a local estate agent to offer a valuation of the property. Every time the poor man came to the farm, the ageing electricity fuse box would inexplicably blow a fuse, leaving the farm in total darkness and without any electricity. This happened more than once and always when he was paying a visit. It seemed that someone, or something, was trying to deter the sale of the farm.

Sarah's grandfather, Sam, could turn his hand to almost any kind of repair and spent a good portion of his time pottering around the farm building gates, fixing fences, replacing windows, painting and generally helping with the upkeep of the farm. He sadly passed away a few years ago having lived well into his 90's. Originally from Liverpool, I enjoyed listening to stories about his family and early life, especially with a single malt whisky in hand. He recalled that he and Sarah's grandmother had settled down one evening whilst they were house sitting. He was sat in the armchair when all of a sudden, and with no warning, a glass lifted itself from the sideboard, slowly moved through the air across the room, and then dropped to the floor, smashing as it hit the stone flagging. As you can imagine, this gave both of them quite a start and Sam said neither of them could explain what had happened. They had clearly seen the glass lift up and float through the air, as if by some unseen hand.

Other members of the family often heard heavy footfalls coming from upstairs when they knew everyone was downstairs. It sounded as if a heavy person, probably a man, was walking along the hallway with metal studded shoes or boots. Interestingly, the footfalls sounded as if they were on stone flags rather than wooden floor boards, obviously harking back to a time before the current flooring was laid. If a member of the family shouted for the entity to stop stomping about, it invariably would! Indeed, the entity used to bang loudly on Sarah's sister's door in the middle of the night until she had had enough and screamed 'Stop it and leave me alone!' ……which it did!

Whilst replacing the aged window frames, Sam noticed a window from the outside of the farm that he couldn't account for, or work out which room it belonged to. He knew the number of rooms on the first floor, and could account for the windows in each room, but this one didn't seem to belong to a room they knew. He concluded it must have been blocked up for some reason, but decided not to start knocking down walls to try to find it and open it up again. Who knows what they would have found in there?

Every single night, around midnight, the pet dogs would start barking at thin air and the cats would sit transfixed, as if staring at some unknown invisible entity. The family often heard strange nocturnal bumps and bangs, but after a while got used to it.

There was a strong residual spirit energy at Boon Kirk Farm. Because of the level of interaction, the entity displayed I would be more inclined to believe there was some intelligence behind the haunting, rather than simply a 'replay' of past events. Who knows whether a previous tenant of Boon Kirk Farm was resting under the cellar, or maybe the entity simply was too attached to the farm to leave? It certainly seemed attached to Sarah's family and kicked up a fuss when they decided to leave!

The Darwen School Apparitions

Source – Staff and Eye Witness

When – January 2019

A wailing woman in black that glides through the canteen and a ghostly boy dressed in Victorian clothes who likes to play the drums! The amazing story of a haunted school built on a once industrial landscape of dark satanic mills and back-to-back mill houses.

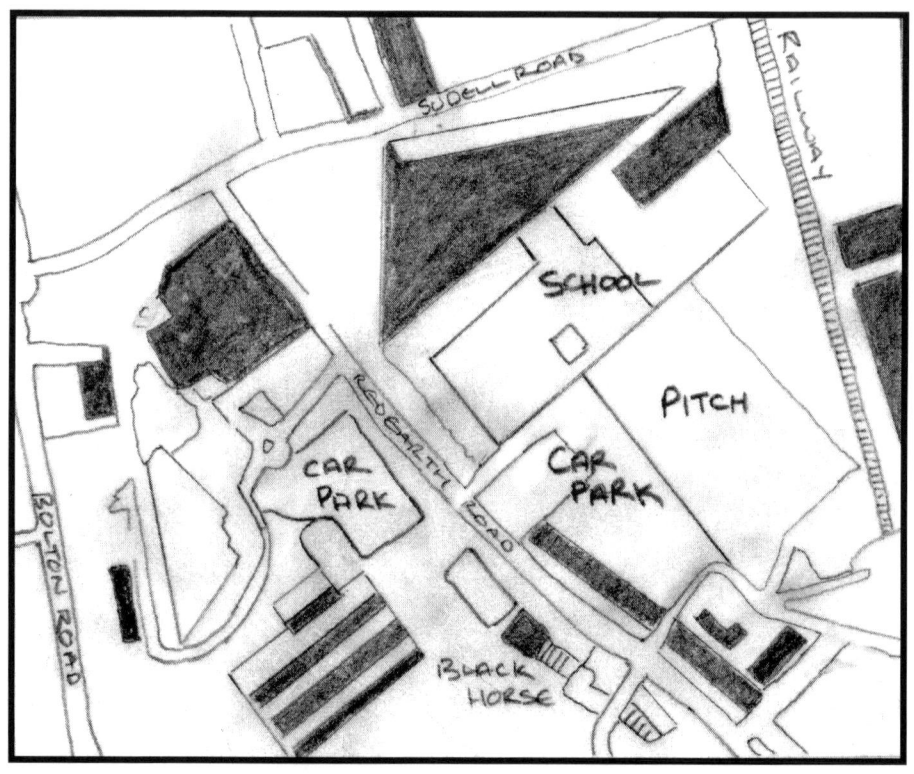

Map of area today © Craig Bryant

Most people would associate a haunting or ghosts with old properties. Simply walking into an old house or building heightens the senses to anything out of the ordinary, and invariably you can find one person who swears there is 'a ghost' attached to the building. Sometimes, however, you hear stories of paranormal activity in the most unlikely of places.

Through a mutual acquaintance, I was introduced to a staff member of a school in Darwen, who had some fascinating stories. The school is a large modern secondary, with over a thousand pupils and is less than 15 years old. Although I was told that some of the teachers and pupils had admitted to witnessing what can only be described as paranormal activity, I agreed I should not name the school due to the nature of some of the activity. I can say that it is situated in Darwen in East Lancashire, and that there was some controversy surrounding the land it was built on.

I decided to conduct some research on the Victorian landscape that the school was built on. A map from the 1890's shows a church on Red Earth Road that is no longer there, and a car park is now built on the graveyard. Hannah Street and Star Street, and the houses on them, are no more. As the stories of the haunting and eye witness accounts unfolded, I began to piece together what, or who, some of these apparitions could be.

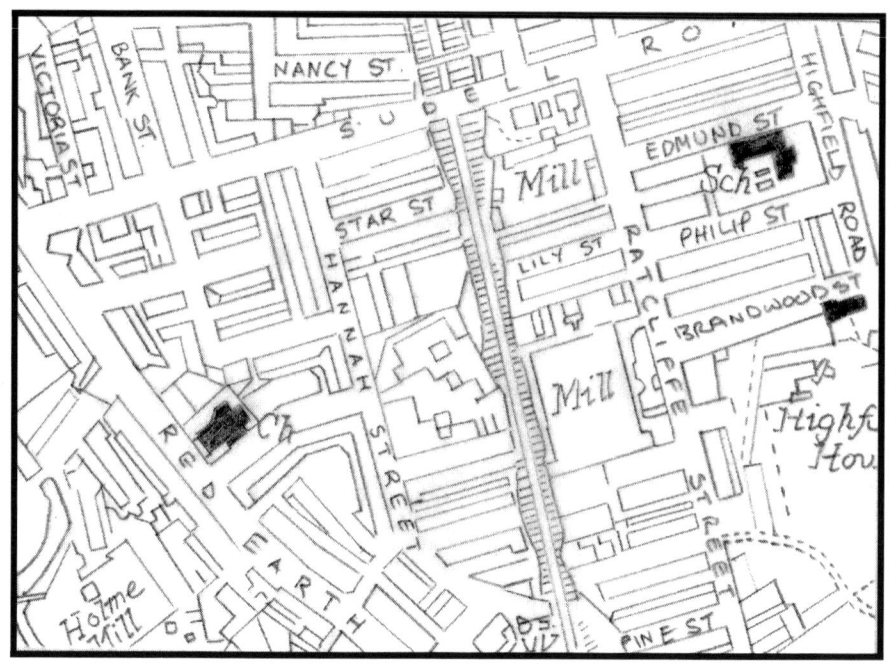

Map of area circa 1890 showing the church and back-to-back houses © Craig Bryant

My source was very credible. On a cold, wet and windy Lancashire Saturday afternoon in January 2019 he agreed to take myself and Sarah on a guided tour of the school, and point out the areas of interest and what he and others had seen. We entered the school and began our tour on the first floor walkway which overlooked a large and airy atrium where the dining area, kitchen and assembly hall were situated.

This central area of the building has huge glass windows around the central 'hub' and a high (three story) ceiling with rows of large lights hanging down some perhaps 20 feet from the ceiling, and at least 30 or 40 feet from the floor. From this central area leads corridors to other parts of the building. The whole concept was designed to give a light, airy and bright feel to the central area of the school, which on entering I felt it succeeded in achieving.

My guide started by explaining the history of the school. Having done some additional research, I discovered that a large number of Victorian Mill houses were demolished to make way for the school, and that a nearby public house was also demolished, leading to a grisly discovery. Buried in the garden the workmen found three skeletons, all in foetal positions, and were later identified as one male, one female and a child. Although the school foundations did not reach as far as the pub, this discovery may have some significance as I will explain later. The real controversy, however, was the removal of a church and graveyard to make way for the building works, and although many bodies were exhumed during the excavations, my guide told me that there was a strong rumour in the community that not all were properly removed.

The number of large lights hanging from the ceiling, maybe a round forty, hung at regular intervals to illuminate the large open canteen and hall area. My guide told me that all the lights were controlled by one switch, so a flick of this switch would turn all the lights on or off simultaneously. However, in the evenings when he goes about his business of locking and securing the school, he and his colleagues had witnessed many times each individual light turning itself on, staying illuminated for several minutes before turning off one by one. If they are already switched on, they will switch themselves off one by one, however, no emergency lighting (designed to come on in the event of an outage of all the lights) would come on. Other lights in the classrooms also randomly turn on and off. He was adamant that there was only himself in the school, as this always happened around 8 o'clock in the evening when he had personally checked the school was empty of pupils or staff. He said the electrical circuits had been checked and there was no explanation for this odd behaviour. Astonishingly, he said that usually at the same time as the lights switching on, the photocopying machine in the hall starts working, and that this can only be switched on with a code typed into a key pad on the machine itself! This is significant because he later described a strange incident which happened in the canteen area, close to where the photocopier is situated.

There are two areas of main activity. One is the kitchen and canteen area and the other is the third floor where the music room is situated. I was led up the third floor by the stairs, as my guide was somewhat reticent to use the lift. He said on many occasions he had been alone in the school and had noticed the lifts going up and down on their own, and on one occasion he had entered the lift on the third floor, near the music room, only to spend the next 10 minutes going up and down several times before finally making the lift stop on the bottom floor, enabling him to get out.

There had been a number of sightings of a little boy dressed in Victorian clothing along this floor, and the sound of drums being played in the music room was a regular occurrence, despite there being nobody in the room. On one occasion, two female pupils were in the girl's toilet on this floor and had taken a selfie, only to see a small boy stood beside them when they looked at the photograph. He was dressed in old Victorian clothes. The two girls had shown the photo to one of the teachers, however, she had left the school at the time I was told the story.

The little boy had been nicknamed 'Caspar' by some of the staff and although many of the staff didn't believe he existed, there were many others who were adamant they had seen or heard him. Interestingly, when the drums were playing on their own, my guide told me the staff often shouted to Caspar and told him to stop, at which point he invariably did!

As we walked around and looked in the music room, I did feel a somewhat oppressive atmosphere, although the corridor was certainly rather narrow compared to other areas we had walked through, and it had quite a low ceiling. The staff member told me of a maintenance engineer who had been working in the vicinity one weekend installing some new CCTV equipment. As he was walking up the stairwell he saw someone walking past the door on the first floor, and knowing there was only himself and my guide in the building (he told me he was nowhere near that stairwell at the time) he went to investigate. Unable to find who it was, he became somewhat concerned and went back to the stairwell and up to the third floor. As he entered the corridor three large ceiling panels spontaneously dropped down in front of him, causing him to shout out in surprise and turn on his heels back down the stairwell. After finding my guide, they both went back to the corridor, and indeed found the panels on the floor, unbroken. The panels were of a thick polystyrene construction, about 18 inches square. As the roof supports where they fell from were still intact, my guide said the only way they could have fallen was to be physically lifted up off the supports and manoeuvred through the gaps. Quite clearly some unknown hand had been at work and had intended to frighten the maintenance worker. Interestingly, a tall dark figure had been seen looking out of the window at the end of this corridor down into the main Atrium of the school and on more than one occasion my guide or one of his colleagues had gone up to the floor to investigate, but were always unable to find anyone there.

The interesting thing about these third floor manifestations is firstly, they seem to be interactive and not just a simple recording. Secondly, being on the third floor, it is unlikely that there would have been a building at the same height there before it was demolished and the school built. Records show two story weavers houses where that part of the school is now built.

Another incident had happened to my guide's teenage daughter who had accompanied him one night on his usual lock-up routine and stayed in the music room to practice on the piano. Nobody else was in the school, and as she was playing she suddenly heard the drums in the next room start to play in time. She stopped, and glanced at the door into the corridor just as a tall dark figure moved past, followed by the handle of the door moving as if someone was trying to get in. By this point scared, she rang her father on his mobile and told him to stop messing about – unfortunately he was outside locking up the all-weather sports pitches! He quickly hurried back inside and found her somewhat shaken, still sat on the piano stool where he had left her some 10 minutes earlier.

As we left the third floor via the stairwell, I noticed how much warmer it was on the stairs than the corridor and music room we had just left. Having worked in modern office blocks it is always noticeable that stairwells are usually colder than the floors they lead to, but not on this occasion. There was a definite temperature drop along the corridor and my guide said that staff and pupils alike had often remarked on freezing cold 'spots' around the music room and corridor. He said that one evening he had finished locking up and had gone up to the staff room to meet another member of staff. As he sat down, he said he suddenly went very cold and felt as if something freezing was hugging him tight. His colleague touched him and was startled at just how cold he felt, yet he said the air temperature felt normal to him. It was simply the area around my guide that was freezing cold. This sensation lasted for a couple of minutes and then slowly subsided, but he said he was quite shaken by the episode.

As we made our way down the canteen and kitchen area, my guide told me of a third apparition that had been seen regularly by both him and many of the staff in the school. One evening, again after locking up as usual, he and two of his colleagues were preparing to settle down for the night in the staffroom when they suddenly heard a woman wailing and screaming, the voice coming from the atrium and canteen area. They quickly went down to see what was happening and as they approached the stairs which led down from the first floor to the ground, he noticed a figure gliding towards the kitchen and disappearing into some ground floor offices. An advertising flag which hung off the wall near to where he saw the figure started fluttering, and as they got to the bottom of the stairs he said an object suddenly whizzed past in front of the three of them from their right and bounced along the floor, hitting one of the windows to their left. He walked over to the object and saw it was a Penny, not an old one but an early Decimalisation Penny. As he bent over to pick it up he said it was so hot he immediately dropped it and couldn't touch if for a good ten minutes as it was just too hot to handle. As they stood looking at the Penny and feeling somewhat intrigued by the activity they had just witnessed, my guide said he saw a small bottle on the floor out of the corner of his eye, and when he walked over to pick it up he said it was smaller than a test tube, clearly quite old with a stopper on the top. He said it did not look modern at all, and in fact looked like an antique. He opened the stopper and smelt strong perfume. He said the bottle was in the middle of the floor when he found it, in plain sight, yet none of them had noticed it earlier despite walking past where it lay as they tried to glimpse the figure they had seen earlier, and that he knew the cleaning staff had been round an hour or so earlier and would have undoubtedly seen it had it fallen out of someone's pocket. It would also have made a noise, or even shattered, if it had landed on the floor tiles from any height.

This particular ghost had been seen a number of times and was described as a woman, dressed in black, wailing and crying as she moved from one side of the atrium to the other. As this part of the school was allegedly built on the church graveyard, it would make sense that this could be a recording of a grieving widow or mother, retracing her footsteps to or from a grave or to the church, obviously wracked with sadness at her loss. My guide said that there is no interaction with this apparition, although a member of the catering staff had apparently seen her floating through the kitchen area during lunchtime and refused to go back in there again. She claimed the woman had no facial features, and as the lady was carrying a tray of food, she dropped it in shock, screamed and ran out vowing never to go in the kitchen again.

An interesting point to note is that there was a lot of opposition to the demolition of the church and exhumation of bodies in the church yard when the ground was being cleared in readiness for building the school. My guide told me that strong rumours persist that not all the bodies were exhumed, and that some remained in the ground when the building started. I have checked through local press reports at the time and although there are a number of stories of locals being both for and against the building (there were a number of condemned houses unfit for habitation which were demolished, much to some local's relief), I can't find any corroboration of this statement. However, from experience of other investigations I have carried out, I feel it is entirely probable. A number of years ago I was researching my family history, and spoke to my Great Aunt, Hilda, sister to my maternal grandfather, who was the last survivor of 11 siblings. She gave me a whole plethora of photographs and personal stories, including one of her sister, Eliza, who died in infancy and was buried in the local churchyard. This was around 1910. The family were very poor; they were mill workers and labourers – 13 in all, including children, and they were crammed into a two – up, two – down terraced house with no indoor bathroom. They could not afford a head stone for Eliza so she was buried in an unmarked grave along the cemetery wall close to the Leeds & Liverpool canal which cut through the town. Hilda told me she knew of several unmarked burials in the graveyard.

It was not uncommon in the 19th and even 20th centuries, especially in the rapidly growing urban industrial conurbations of Lancashire, to be so poor that a family could not afford a simple headstone to mark the grave of a loved one. It is entirely possible that this practice persisted across parishes, and that the church in this story was no different. I would be surprised if all the remains were exhumed, simply because burials were sometimes unmarked and often unrecorded.

As we were shown into the kitchen area of the school, I was immediately struck by how oppressive it felt and as I stood in there for a few minutes I began to feel very 'down', almost upset for no apparent reason. I also had a sensation of feeling dizzy and rocking from side to side like being on a boat. It was a very peculiar feeling and it was only after we had left the room that I was told the 'Wailing Lady' had been seen many times in that area, and that the member of kitchen staff who had seen the apparition saw her gliding through the wall from the canteen area into the kitchen we had just been stood in. Although I do not consider myself psychic, in that I do not purport to talk to spirits, on occasions I have picked up on negative energy whilst in a building or a room and there was a definite concentration of something unpleasant in the kitchen and canteen areas. It was a most peculiar feeling I had whilst stood in the kitchen. It was a feeling of great sadness and physical instability. This particular part of the school had been built on land which was previously part of the graveyard.

As our tour continued, we were led away from the canteen down a corridor to a number of classrooms. Each classroom felt the same, eerie (I was a little shaken by what had happened in the canteen) but nonetheless devoid of any activity. It was only when we entered the last classroom on the corridor that things began to feel strange again.

This room was a triangular shape, peculiar for a classroom. As I entered the room I immediately felt there was a strong male presence. I was drawn to the apex of the room and as I stood in the corner I immediately felt the same dizziness and rocking motion that I had in the kitchen. Our guide told us that this part of the building was also where the graveyard had been, and that successive teachers who had used this room had all felt uncomfortable, some to the point that they blocked off the apex with boxes or a whiteboard to stop themselves and others from having to go into that part of the room. At this point, Sarah said she had begun to feel uncomfortable, and that she had suddenly started thinking about two names – John and Robert. It was somewhat of a relief to leave the room and make our way back to the main hall and the entrance. As we walked along the corridor, the staff member told me that a number of other colleagues had witnessed strange occurrences, notably one evening when two of them were locking up the all-weather sports pitches, one turned to look across the school yard and noticed a dark figure looking at them through a third floor window. They hurried back across the yard to establish who it was – they had done a full circle of the school previously and they were convinced nobody was left in the building. As they entered the building they agreed to split up, one went clockwise around the building and the other anti-clockwise, planning to meet at the staff room. When they both got their, neither had been able to find anyone, and on checking the CCTV they clearly saw themselves moving around the building but there was absolutely no sign of anyone else.

There are a number of observations about this haunting that it is worth considering.

The three apparitions seemed quite different. Certainly 'Caspar' and the 'Shadow Man' seemed more interactive than the 'Wailing Lady'. They are both particularly active on the third floor and there are personal testimonies of objects being moved, drums being played and actual photographic evidence. There are also a number of people who have witnessed these phenomena, from staff, pupils, a workman and staff family members. 'Caspar' seems playful whilst the 'Shadow Man' would seem to be a more threatening presence and may have been responsible for the ceiling collapse witnessed by the CCTV fitter.

The 'Wailing Lady' on the other hand is an interesting phenomenon. At first I considered she may be a 'recording', a flashback to a traumatic time where the apparition was so wracked with grief that somehow this negative energy has imprinted it self on the very ground that used to be the graveyard, and continues to manifest itself in the building that has since been built above it. This doesn't, however, explain the spontaneous throwing of a scalding hot coin or the sudden appearance of an old perfume bottle in the middle of the floor shortly after a sighting. Looking at the old map of the area from 1890 it is clear that the church and graveyard are no longer there, and that a car park has now been built over the area where the graveyard would have been. This corroborates the first part of the story. Both Hannah Street and Star Street have gone, along with the houses that were on them. I believe that the Wailing Lady is following the path of Hannah Street south towards where the church and graveyard would have been. She must, therefore, have been a resident of the houses along these roads now demolished.

The railway line passes close to the now demolished houses, with two large mills on the other side of the tracks. However, the map shows a strange unnamed building in-between Hannah Street and the railway, right where the school is built. Perhaps this is why 'Caspar' keeps appearing in the music room corridor. From the map, it is impossible to tell how many stories it had but perhaps it was a tall building at the height of its modern replacement? That would explain why Caspar is an active ghost, on the third floor of a modern building.

Finally, the physical effect that certain parts of the building had on us was quite alarming. It would be easy for a sceptic to say that because I had been pre-warned of the paranormal activity in the building, I was more likely to think something was out of the ordinary or more likely to see or hear something that wasn't actually there. I approached this investigation with an open mind and had no preconception of what might happen during our walk round. What I felt was a sense of sadness and a feeling of physical disorientation, particularly in two places, which both took me by surprise. I felt there was a strong negative feeling in these areas and that there was something unpleasant in the fabric of the building or emanating from the floor below. The paranormal activity in this place is truly fascinating.

A Fond Farewell?

When – 2008

Source – Family member

An unseen, ghostly hand gently stroking a baby's back under a vest, the outline of the fingers clearly visible. It was a heart stopping moment. Was it sinister, or simply a fond farewell?

2008 was particularly sad year for me and my family. We lost two very close friends within 3 months of each other, both were aged 40 and both passed away suddenly. As I write this book, 11 years on, I still feel a huge sense of loss and sadness, and the impact it had on their families and friends.

Dave passed away at the age of 40. He was Godparent to my son James and amongst other hobbies, an avid collector of films. A few weeks after the funeral we were invited to his widow's house along with a group of his other friends to help go through his vast collection of DVD's (and some video cassettes) and help box them up to take to a local charity shop.

The atmosphere was sombre although we tried to be cheerful. Dave had passed away in the house and somehow I felt as if he were still there. I had the strangest feeling he hadn't moved on, and I was about to be proved right.

Sarah and I had taken James with us and, as he was not yet two years old, he became tired and needed a lie down. Sarah asked if she could take him for a nap in the main bedroom and proceeded to strip him down to his vest, lay him on the bed and gently stroke his head to help him relax and fall asleep. As she was doing this, she said she saw his vest ripple and the outline of a hand gently appear under the vest, making a gentle stroking motion over James as he lay there. Sarah said she was utterly astonished, but as she watched the outline of the hand for a few seconds, she said she didn't feel any alarm and James didn't seem distressed or bothered at all. After a few seconds, the shape of the hand slowly moved away and Sarah sat there for a moment contemplating what she had just seen. She stayed with James for a while but, despite being a very protective mummy, she said she had no worry about leaving him in the bedroom on his own whilst she rejoined me and the rest of our friends. There were no other incidents that evening, although I sensed that Dave was there in some form, and that if there is an afterlife, he came to say goodbye before moving on. We visited his widow a number of times in the months that followed before sadly losing touch.

I often think about Dave, and wonder whether his presence is still in the house.

A Clayton-Le-Moors Haunting and Pit Disaster.

Source – Eye Witness

When – 2001 to approximately 2011

The ghosts of trapped miners and a remorseful pit supervisor, spectral children and a malevolent priest haunt this family home. A house in Clayton-Le-Moors, built over a long disused mine shaft, harboured literally dozens of ghosts.

Whilst researching this book, I was contacted by a lady called Susan who told me the most astonishing story of a house she lived in for 10 years. The house was part of an old farmhouse, she believed it was converted from stables, and situated down a quiet unmade road in Clayton-Le-Moors near to Accrington called 'Chequers'. I spoke to her at length about her experiences and this is the account she gave:

"We moved into the house in July 2001. We did the house up before we moved in, whilst we were renovating it we heard noises and bangs but we didn't take any notice. When we moved in, we had a safety gate at the top of the stairs. From the first night we lived there, in the early hours we heard footsteps walking up the stairs and then we heard the safety gate being shaken. We then heard footsteps along the landing, followed by the bathroom door opening and we heard what we thought was the light switch being turned on.

My husband got up, thinking it was one of our children walking about in the early hours and wanted to check on them to make sure they were ok. When he checked, all the children were fast asleep in bed, so he went downstairs to check everything was ok down there. He found everything was exactly as it was when we went to bed.

Every night without fail the same thing happened. We got use to it eventually and learnt to ignore it. However, after a while we started to hear running upstairs in the back bedroom and landing, even the light shade was shaking in the room below, the footsteps were that heavy. I went upstairs and there was no one there. I was the only one in the house, my husband was at work, my children were at school and nursery. This started to happen every day; again we got use to it and learnt to ignore it. One day I heard my son talking to someone in his room, so I went in to see who he was talking to but there was no one there. I asked him who he was talking to and he said he was talking to two girls. I could not see anyone else in the room, so I asked him to describe them to me. My son said they were wearing Victorian clothes and that their names were Christie and Helener, Christie was 11 and Helener was 9 and that they use to live here. My son said they played 'Hide and Seek' and 'Ring a Ring of Roses' but when anyone else comes upstairs they stop and hide. I asked my son how long he had been friends with them and he said not long, only shortly after we moved in the house. I figured he just had pretend friends, so I didn't ask him anything more about it.

One day, my husband and I were stood in the door way of the kitchen, talking to our eldest son, when in front of our very eyes, a pair of scissors that were on the table next to the sofa flew across the room straight at our son, who was sat down in the chair. Fortunately, our son was not injured, as it had just missed him but he was very shook up, as we all were.

It was at this point nasty things began to happen. One day my husband and I were sat in the middle room watching the television with the children upstairs. We then heard running about in the back bedroom, but as I said before, we were use to it. On this occasion my husband went upstairs to see what was happening. As he got to the top of the stairs, he went towards the door of our eldest son's room. As he approached, the door slammed shut in his face, and it was slammed so hard that it split the wood up the middle of the door. There was no explanation for this, there were no windows open and we couldn't feel a draft. My husband came back downstairs shaking. After that, I was hit on the head with a football boot stud, which was on the table next to where my husband was sat. We both saw it rise up and shoot across the room. That was the final straw. I contacted our local priest and asked him to perform an exorcism. Unfortunately, that didn't work and it only seemed to make things worse.

I decided to contact a local medium. On the night before she was due to visit the house, we were in bed and suddenly the wardrobe door swung wide open and then slammed itself shut.

When the medium came to visit, she told us that we had 13 spirits in total. One was a priest called Matthew who was actually very evil and the other spirits were scared of him. I have done some research and it seems he was somehow involved as a priest at nearby Dunkenhalgh Hall in the 1500's and that he had a reputation of being a bad man. She said she could feel that Helena and Christie were very frightened of Matthew, as were many of the other spirits that were attached to the house.

Some of the spirits were men who had been killed in an explosion at the coal mine at Moorfield Colliery at Altham, near Accrington in 1883. Part of the mine workings went under the street where my house was and when the explosion happened there were a number of miners trapped underneath. From talking to three other neighbours, their houses had entities attached to them as well, although my house seemed to be the one with the most activity. I was told two girls had died in our house in a fire, after their mother had left them on their own whilst she nipped to the shop. The girls were upstairs in their bedroom, which was the 'back bedroom' as we call it, but it was bigger in the past because our house and next door use to be one big farm house. The girls had been playing a game running around the bedroom when one of them knocked a candle over, and that is how the fire started. Incidentally, we forever smelt burning and we would get up in the middle of the night convinced the house was on fire. I was talking to our neighbour one day, who had lived in her house from the 1940's and she told me she could smell burning in her middle room at the back of the TV. We could smell burning at the back of our middle room, which is next to the dividing wall between our houses. I could not believe it - this explained why we could smell burning all the time! The medium told us the street was full of spirits and that they had tried to move on. She said she had a message for me from the men who were killed in the pit disaster. They said that they were murdered and that the truth needed to come out. The medium told me they wanted me to get proof that they had been murdered in the pit accident. It dawned on me that they couldn't move on because of the way they had sadly died. I didn't know what to say, so I tried to explain that there was nothing I could do, because the explosion and disaster had happened over 100 years ago.

A few months later, my husband had been working in a house and had been given a few books about the area to give to me, knowing my love of local history. One of the books was about the mining disaster, which went into detail about what had happened. The book told of how the men had gone to work as normal and when they went down into the pit, they were hit with a smell of gas. The miners who were nearest to the pit head got into the cage and were pulled up to the pit head. The foreman was at the pit head and demanded to know why they had come back up. The Miners told him they could smell gas and by this time there were more Miners at the bottom of the pit screaming for them to drop the cage so that they could get out. The Foreman refused to open the cage to let the Miners out and dropped the cage back down into the Pit Shaft! The cage jammed and couldn't be moved so the Foreman panicked, ordering the doors to be shut and ran for his life. As he was running away from the Pit Head there was an enormous explosion and he was seriously injured in the blast. All the Miners who were trapped in the pit and the cage died in the explosion and many more at the Pit Head were injured.

An inquest was quickly carried out into what had happened, and the Foreman was required to give evidence. By this time the Foreman was barely alive and at home in bed suffering terribly from his injuries. They needed his testimony so all of the Jury and the Judge, together with all their entourage, went to his home to try to find out what had happened. I was gobsmacked when I realised it was my address! I could not believe what I was reading. I realised it explained why the ghosts of the Miners were stuck in my house and believed the Foreman was guilty of murder by his actions. Not long after this, we moved from the house, but I believe the paranormal activity is so bad that no one will live in the house longer than 6 months. "

The Moorfield Colliery disaster of 1883 claimed the lives of 55 men and 13 boys, all of school age. Contemporary reports give the following sad stories of just some of the victims of that horrific day: -

Mrs Almond, who was a widow, lost two sons that day. John was aged 20, and Cuthbert was just 12. The following May another son George, who had been badly burned in the explosion, died in hospital after suffering an overdose of chloroform while having a tooth extracted.

David Cronshaw had the awful task of identifying his three sons: Jackson, James (who was married with 3 children) and Thomas. He also had another son badly injured. Sadly, this was not the first time that tragedy had struck the Cronshaw family as they had already lost one son in another pit accident, another son was drowned in the local Leeds Liverpool canal and the previous year, their daughter, Jane, had also died.

James Clegg was helping to wash the bodies so that they could be identified. He failed to recognise his own son William who had been badly burned. His wife was called in to help with the horrible task and recognised a scar on her son's chest where she had recently applied a mustard plaster (an old remedy for chest infections and bad coughs). The Clegg's also lost another son George and two brothers.

Thirteen of the dead were children under the age of 16.

11 year old Henry Crossley died on what unbelievably was the third day he had worked there. 13 year old Michael Mahon survived the explosion and was on his way out of the pit when he turned back to search for his 15 year old brother John, both were later found dead. Thomas Edge was 14 and was carried out of the pit by his father. He died three days later. His older brother, John, who was 16, was also killed in the disaster.

James Macintosh was the under-manager at the colliery. He was the first man down the mine after the explosion and spent the next 24 hours underground helping the injured and searching for the dead, one of whom was his father, Thomas Macintosh, the colliery manager. James was later offered the management of the colliery, which he declined and he never went down the mine again. James later became the landlord of a pub called the Greyhound Hotel on Whalley Road in Accrington, close to Clayton-Le-Moors and Altham. On the morning of the 10th anniversary of the disaster, James came downstairs into the public bar and committed suicide.

Between 1880 and 1890, there were no less than 22 major pit disasters in Britain, resulting in the deaths of 1,741 men and boys, many of them as young as ten years old. To establish why the disaster happened in the first place, it is worth looking at the history of the Colliery, and the horrific conditions in which men and boys were expected to work in order to help fuel Britain's expanding heavy industries. It may help explain why many of the poor souls trapped down the mine that day cannot move on, and echoes of the past permeate through the row of cottages that still stand today.

The Colliery was originally named 'Altham Colliery' and it is not known when it became 'Moorfield Colliery'. It is situated on the A678 Blackburn to Burnley Road, near to Padiham. The mine was initially worked as a single shaft pit, the shaft being divided down the centre by a 'brattice' (a wooden partition with the seams between the planks sealed with pitch). Air would travel down one side of the brattice, circulate around the workings, and return up the other side. This was just one of several ways of creating a circulation of air, as well as furnaces and windmills.

The Colliery was built above two seams of coal – 'Upper Mountain' and 'Lower Mountain'. The workings were extensive, and ran under Clayton-Le-Moors and along to Blackburn some 10 miles away. It was said a man could walk from the pit head to Blackburn uninterrupted. The shafts also connected another local mine on Whinney Hill in Accrington, now the site of a landfill. The Upper Mountain seam was thinner and soon exhausted, meaning the Colliery owners had to consent to deeper shafts being sunk in order to access the thicker, but deeper, Lower Mountain seam. The colliery was owned by W. E. Taylor of the newly formed Altham Colliery Company. In 1868, the company was taken over by a partnership between James Barlow, the second Mayor of Accrington and J. J. Rippon, who also had an interest in the Great Harwood Colliery Co. The company also owned the Martholme and Whinney Hill collieries. All these Collieries were with a few miles of each other, and the underground warren of mine workings still exist today. Subsidence is a huge problem, a good example being the length of Burnley Road in Accrington which reputedly has a shaft running directly below it. James Barlow bought out Rippon's interest in the company in 1868 and extended his mining interests further when he bought out the Rippon family's interests in the Great Harwood Colliery Company in 1892. Collieries were seen purely as a means of income and, preceding any Health and Safety legislation, huge risks were often taken to access the richest seams.

In 1862, at the Hartley Colliery, near Newcastle-upon-Tyne, the cast iron beam of the pumping engine broke away and fell into the shaft, taking the brattice and cage with it. The shaft was completely sealed, thereby entombing 204 men and boys. In 1864, a law was passed outlawing single shaft mines. As with many Acts of Parliament, the owners found ways to avoid complying with them. Numerous single shaft mines were still working years after the Act was passed. Many of the owners claimed they could not justify the cost of sinking a second shaft, and they would have to work the mine until it could be linked-up with the workings of another colliery. This could have been the case at Moorfield and the reason why it was linked to Whinney Hill.

It was around 1868 that the shaft at Moorfield was taken down a further 173 feet to the Lower Mountain seam, which was about 28 inches thick. Two stone drifts, 8-foot-wide and 7-foot-high, were driven 1,200 yards from the base of the shaft to the shaft at Whinney Hill. One of the drifts, known by the miners as 'Billy Brow', became the main haulage road, along which ran the chain haulage system. It was powered by a twin-cylinder steam engine situated at the base of the Whinney Hill shaft. The other drift, the return airway for both collieries, was the road for the miners to walk to and from the Coal Face. The roadway was a 1 in 6 incline and there were 264 steps cut into the floor to help the men to climb it. Originally there was a metal handrail down the centre of the road, to separate the men coming on shift from those going off. This enabled the men to pass each other without getting in each other's way.

The cause of the explosion was a deadly combination of methane gas and coal dust. On the morning of the 7th November 1883, when the first of the men descended the shaft at Moorfield Colliery, they entered an atmosphere which was like a bomb waiting to explode. In one of the headings off the No. 2 level, gas was seeping from a fault in the coalface, which had been cut into the rock. Four hours later this gas was ignited by the miners own Davy Safety Lamps, which initially ignited the coal dust. The coal dust itself had accumulated over the years, coating the walls, roof and timbers from the pit face to the shaft. The explosion happened with a terrible force.

For many years in the main room of the Greyhound Hotel at Altham West, there was a framed list of those who lost their lives in the disaster. In 1994 this list was removed to Altham parish church. A local calligrapher, Terry Woods from Oswaldtwistle, created an illuminated scroll of the dead, which is now in the library at Clayton-le-Moors.

A plaque can be found on Pilkington's Bridge in Altham West, known locally as Dickie Brig, which commemorates the 110th anniversary of the disaster and was laid in October 1993 by a former Hyndburn Mayor, Councillor Mrs. Cathleen Thom.

Coal mining ended at Whinney Hill in 1932. The shafts were left open to ventilate the workings at Moorfield but they were later filled in and capped off. A large housing estate has been built on the land once occupied by Whinney Hill colliery, and the NORI brick works (a history lesson in itself – NORI bricks were famous the world over). The site of the shafts can be found on the right of the road going up to Whinney Hill from the traffic lights at the Greyhound Hotel. Directly above the entrance to the estate a small area has been fenced off and trees have been planted directly over the shafts.

In 1948, the year after the nationalisation of the coal industry, work in the Lower Mountain seam ceased. In 1949 the workings in the Upper Mountain seam were abandoned, bringing years of coal production at Moorfield to an end. The shaft has been capped off but not filled in.

Whilst researching this sad story I found numerous eye witness accounts of the aftermath of the explosion, but little about what happened shortly before or during. Having spoken to Susan, however, I have no doubt of the validity of her story and the tragic loss of life that ensued during and after the explosion. I have no doubt that such an event has left its mark on the very fabric of the area, and with a shaft running directly under, with the deaths of so many men, it must surely have left its mark on the houses above. I have no doubt that the houses have a number of entities unable to move on, endlessly searching for justice after having their lives cut so tragically short.

Wood Terrace

Source – Author

When – 2006 - 2007

A ghostly lady in the night, distant lullabies and two sisters who didn't want us to leave. This 19th century weaver's cottage had a fascinating presence.

The experiences I had at Wood Terrace never felt threatening. I do not recall having any bad feelings about the fabric of the house at all, in fact, quite the opposite. With its Victorian surround open fire in the lounge, it was, and still is, one of the comfiest, most welcoming houses I have ever lived in, especially on a stormy Lancashire night!

One of a row of six terraced cottages, Wood Terrace is situated in the village of Chatburn, just outside Clitheroe. Built in the 1880's it was originally a cotton weavers house and census records show its first occupants were two sisters and their family from Ashton-Under-Lyne, Manchester, who moved to work in the local Cotton Mill. The census records showed no adult male living in the property. A typical small cottage, it had an open coal fire in the lounge, kitchen at the rear and two upstairs bedrooms. A bathroom had been added which thankfully made the outside toilet redundant. Behind where the outside toilet was (now a utility room) is a funeral directors and undertakers!

After our son James was born, Sarah and I noticed a few odd things happening in the house. Until he was about 6 months old, James slept in a cot by our bed in the main bedroom. We used to put a small light by the side on the cot on the floor so that the room was dimly lit, bright enough to see during nocturnal feeds (James was a hungry baby and used to wake every couple of hours) but not too bright as to keep us awake. We only had one pet at that time, a cat called Tigger, who used to sleep under the cot next to the light, as it was obviously warm.

I recall James was a few months old and found myself becoming a lighter and lighter sleeper. Sarah and I used to take turns feeding him and one particular night I woke up from a light sleep to see, to my surprise, a shadowy figure leaning over James's cot as if looking down at him. This lasted for a few seconds, long enough for me to panic, but I didn't. Strangely, I felt only calm and benevolence from whatever the spirit was that stood by his cot. Within seconds the figure disappeared. Although it was quite translucent, I remember to this day that the figure seemed to be that of an elderly woman. I told Sarah about the incident the following day, and although healthily sceptical (as I am) she didn't dismiss the story out of hand.

James was born in October, and the following summer another incident occurred that both I and Sarah witnessed. In this case it was an audible phenomenon, and we were both quite taken aback. In fact, when I told her I was writing this book, she reminded me not to leave this story out.

As I mentioned, the house was old and it used to have an outdoor toilet, or 'Cludgy' as my grandmother used to call it. I remember my maternal grandmother having an outside toilet in her terraced house in Accrington right up to the late 1960's when they had an indoor toilet and bath fitted. This made the tin bath in front of the fire somewhat redundant. In the case of Wood Terrace, the outside toilet had been converted into a utility room where the freezer and washing machine were now kept, and accessed across a communal alley that ran along the back of the row of houses. None of the houses had rear gardens, although we did fill up plenty of pots and even old chimney stacks with flowers of all sorts that looked lovely during the summer months.

One summer's evening I went out to the utility room and as I was unloading the washing machine, I heard the faint echoes of a woman singing. It is difficult to describe what it sounded like, but although it was obviously coming from close by, it also somehow sounded distant, almost from another time. The singing was very gentle, and as I listened, I could make out the words to 'Twinkle, Twinkle Little Star'. Now, the thing to bear in mind is that out of the six cottages we were the only one with a young child, in fact, two of the houses had elderly ladies living in them, two had single men and the fifth a middle aged lady who didn't have grandchildren or young children herself. I was convinced therefore that the singing wasn't coming from any of the other houses on the row. In addition, it was a young girls voice, faint but distinctive. As I walked out and back onto the alleyway the singing stopped. I quickly locked the door and hurried back into the house where Sarah was sat watching the TV. I started to tell her what had just happened when she interrupted me (not for the first time!), and said that she too had heard distant singing and that she could make out the words to a nursery rhyme – 'Twinkle, Twinkle Little Star'. Of course, at this point we both ran upstairs to check James was ok, and of course he was. He was fast asleep.

Sarah mentioned these phenomena to our elderly neighbour, who had lived in her house next door all her life. She had been born there and carried on living in the house when her parents passed away. She told us that her two Spinster Aunts had lived in our house for many years before a gentleman by the name of Albert bought it. She showed us an old black and white photograph of them both standing outside our house and told us they were both buried in the local church yard. Sarah would often take James out for long walks in his pram and used to called at the church to visit their grave, just to say 'Hello'.

The final incident was very interesting to say the least. Due to our growing family, and lack of storage space in a two up – two down terraced cottage, we decided to move house. My mother was still living in Accrington, and as we had lost my dad to cancer some years earlier, she lived alone and decided she wanted to move closer to us. We luckily found a house in the village which needed some restoration, so my Mother agreed to buy Wood Terrace. I remember one afternoon I was packing some things away in boxes in the kitchen, Sarah was at work and James was at nursery. I had taken a few days off work to get on top of the packing and as I was filling boxes with plates and cutlery all of a sudden, all hell broke loose in the main bedroom directly above where I was in the kitchen. To say that it sounded like several heavy-footed people stomping about was an understatement. I immediately ran upstairs thinking that somehow burglars had managed to get past me and up the stairs, but on entering the bedroom there was nothing, including the noise which had stopped as quickly as it started.

I went back downstairs and carried on packing, when no sooner had I put the next plate in the box than the banging and heavy footfalls started again! At this point, despite feeling somewhat unnerved I shouted at the top of my voice 'Stop doing that! Yes, we are leaving the house, but my Mother is moving in and you know her, because she's been here lots of times…. now BEHAVE!'

The commotion stopped immediately. I remember standing in the kitchen and looking up at the ceiling for several minutes but everything remained calm. I carried on doing my packing, thankfully in silence.

The house sale went through and we moved, on the same day my Mother moved into Wood Terrace. I have asked her a few times whether she's encountered anything peculiar in the house, but she just shakes her head and says 'No'. Perhaps she's not tuned in the same way I or Sarah are, or perhaps she's just not telling!

Wood Terrace is fascinating because the manifestations were very real. Whether they were of the first or later occupants of the house would be impossible to say but they were very real, and very active.

Curry's Electrical Shop, Oldham

Source –Author

When – Mid 1980's

An atmosphere of dread and sadness and furtive shadows. The ghost of a man who hanged himself lingers in the third floor stockroom.

In the late 1980's I spent a few years working in electrical retail. Curry's were an electrical retail group, owned by Dixons PLC, and at that time were mainly high street shops, often in old buildings situated on high streets up and down the country. The shop in Oldham was no different. Sadly, it is no longer there as around that time retailers were closing high street stores in favour of large, out of town, Superstores, a trend which sadly continues today.

I had transferred to the Oldham store from Middleton, a small town on the north side of Manchester close to the M66 motorway, in the days before the M60 ring road was completed. Oldham, on the other hand, is a town to the North East of Manchester, high on the moors near to the M62 motorway and Saddleworth, a name which conjures up unpleasant images and memories for many in the North of England.

Oldham itself is a town that like many in the North, has suffered from its fair share of economic downturns over the years. Like many Lancashire towns it was heavily reliant on Cotton and following the collapse of the industry after the Second World

War, Oldham struggled to maintain its prosperous past. Certainly, when I was there in the late 1980's the town was a shadow of its former grandeur. Although it was obvious from its splendid, if faded, architecture and buildings, that it had once been a prosperous and thriving community, the town had obviously seen better days. Many of its former Municipal Buildings had been closed and were now occupied by cheap retail outlets and charity shops. Buildings left to decay and a general air of lack of prosperity meant it wasn't the most cheerful of places to work. Although Lancashire people are, in general, most accommodating and friendly (certainly more so than that miserable lot across the Pennines!), economic hardship and depression takes its toll on communities and Oldham, like so many other Lancashire towns, suffered the same fate. Sadly, even though I am recalling events of almost 30 years ago, nothing has changed for towns like Oldham.

I was asked to transfer to the Oldham Branch to drive the delivery van after one of the drivers had misjudged the height of the box van and driven under a low bridge that was a foot shorter than the van. Being a young lad in my early twenties, it was great fun being out on the road all day rather than being stuck on a stuffy shop floor selling toasters to old ladies and extolling the virtues of Twin Tubs over these new-fangled automatic washing machines.

The shop was a three-story building, in the middle of a row of similar buildings most of which had also been converted into shops. The façade looked Victorian. The ground floor was where the shop front was, with its displays of washing machines, fridge freezers, televisions, video recorders and a new invention called 'compact disc players' which were causing quite a stir. One of the first music CD's to be released was Dire Straits 'Brothers in Arms' album and we used it to demonstrate the crystal-clear clarity of CD's over those old-fashioned records people had been playing for years. Funny how turntables are making a comeback as I write this collection of stories, but that's a whole different subject! I have to say that every time I hear Mark Knoffler's fabulous guitar riff at the beginning of 'Money for Nothing' it takes me right back to my younger days!

At the back of the shop was the managers office, and on the first floor a couple of small store rooms, a kitchen, toilet facilities and repair shop for those items that could be repaired on site rather than sent back to the manufacturer. The shop also had a lift which was used to move heavier items, such as washing machines and fridge freezers, between floors. Imagine a 'Dumb Waiter' only bigger. It was, however, the third floor which was to be the most interesting.

The whole of the third floor was used as a stock room. I don't recall the dimensions of the room but it was fairly large, given that at least a third of it was taken up with a huge floor to ceiling cage where the high value goods would be stored, and locked away at night in case of a break in or robbery. Items such as video recorders, CD players, camcorders, and satellite receivers would be stored in the cage as well as other high value items such as the more expensive Walkmans and personal stereos. Basically, anything that could be easily transported and sold off the back of a lorry. It did happen! Items would habitually go missing from the shop floor and I remember once someone actually stole a washing machine that had been chained to a door post at the front of the shop, during opening hours, in broad daylight!

The building itself was old and had a dark atmosphere to it. The ground floor didn't feel too bad however, it was light and had two large glass doors at the front that opened to the outside and always had people around, whether it was staff or customers. The second floor felt more oppressive and unpleasant but the third floor was truly terrifying. I always felt uncomfortable when I was up there, the air was heavy and it felt cold, even on the warmest of days outside. It was musty and smelt damp and dust hung heavy in the air. There was only one window at the end of the room, so it was dark and unwelcoming. Even turning the lights on didn't make it feel any better. It felt like somewhere a demonic spirit would hide – little did I know.

I distinctly remember the first time I went up to the third floor alone. I had been shown around by the manager on the day I transferred to the shop, and I remember feeling uneasy as he was explaining how to unlock the cage and make sure it was secure again, going on and on about security and break-ins and the local shoplifters and stock counts and so on. As you can imagine my mind was wandering a little, not because he was boring me in particular and 'teaching me how to suck eggs' as we say in Lancashire, but that I felt distinctly uneasy being in the room. I thought little of it at the time and continued on my whistle-stop tour of the facilities with the manager, who I distinctly remember, was a rather jovial and good-natured bloke. All this changed however after I had returned from my first trip to the third floor alone.

I had been asked by the manager to go up to the third floor and bring a boxed video recorder down. I remember walking into the stock room and immediately thought how cold it felt compared to the stairwell I had just walked up. As I walked across the room towards the cage at the far end, I remember feeling a sudden and quite alarming sense of fear. This sense suddenly hit me for no discernable reason, and I could feel myself going colder with goose bumps on my arms and a sense of oppression that I remember to this day. The whole room felt as if it was closing in on me and I knew I was not alone in the room. Something was in there with me and it was terrifying. I thought I saw something moving in the shadows, crouched, distorted, and evil.

I very quickly unlocked the cage door, retrieving the item and quickly locking it and hurrying out of the room. By this point I was hot and sweating and I felt dizzy and very unwell. I quickly gathered myself and went down the stairs and stopped at the bottom to catch my breath, just as the manager was walking past. I handed him the box and he gave me a quizzical look. I told him I didn't like it up there and that something had made me feel uneasy and scared. He stared at me for a moment and asked me what I had seen. I replied I had seen nothing, as such, just that I had a bad feeling when I went into the stockroom and that it just didn't 'feel right' somehow. I didn't want to mention the shadow in case he thought I was mad. He didn't say anything, and after a moment of staring at me, which was off putting on its own, he turned and walked back onto the shop floor.

A few days later I was chatting with the lady who dealt with all the returned faulty items. She worked out of a small office on the second floor, piled high with bubble wrapped returns waiting to be collected by the delivery drivers and returned to the distribution centre. I don't recall how we got on to the subject, but I mentioned how uncomfortable I had felt going up to the third-floor stockroom on my own, and how it felt really cold and oppressive.

To my astonishment, my colleague proceeded to explain that I was lucky I hadn't seen the figure of a man with a noose around his neck, swinging in mid air! She went on to explain the shop had been there for years and that she had witnessed a female member of staff a few years previous come running down the stairs screaming about a ghost, and proceeded to put her coat on and run out of the shop never to return. She continued she been told about the apparition by the previous manager when he left the shop and that she knew of at least two other staff members who had seen what they described as 'something strange' up there and left shortly afterwards. Although she hadn't seen the apparition herself, she said she knew how I felt being up there alone as she too had experienced similar feelings of dread

.

The incident left me very shaken, and I refused to go back to the storeroom on my own, a request the manager was happy to grant. He obviously knew something, but was not saying!

I never quite got over the feeling of oppression and dread that I had felt that day and the whole incident tainted my time working at Curry's in Oldham, despite the Manager and the staff I worked with being some of the nicest people I have ever had the pleasure to meet. When I was offered the chance to become mobile and travel around different shops as a Relief Manager I jumped at the chance, not just because it was a promotion but because it meant I could leave the Oldham shop. I worked at many different shops after that, some in buildings that had a particular feel about them, but none with quite the oppressive atmosphere of the Oldham shop.

Having thought about the incident over the years, perhaps the 'haunting' in this case is a type of recording, being played back time and time again with the feelings of depression and fear heightened after years of being trapped within the walls of the building. Perhaps what happened in the past was so traumatic that some sort of residual energy has been left behind, or perhaps there is a Time Slip opening a window to that horrific moment in time. Perhaps the feeling of isolation the poor victim felt has somehow translated into energy that you can only feel when you too are alone in the room. Whatever the reason, it felt very real to me and other people who ventured up to the third floor alone.

Most of Curry's high street stores have now closed, preferring to relocate to out of town retail parks and superstores. I have no idea what became of the building in Oldham, whether it still stands or whether it still operates as a retail outlet of some sort. Maybe, one day, I will go back and try to find it. I will most certainly never forget it!

The Little Boy With No Legs

Source – Home Owner

When – Present Day

The ghost of a little boy with no legs who plays with the owner's daughter, and an eerie disembodied voice…...

Front of the house. Photograph taken by the owner. © Craig Bryant

The more I talk to people about ghosts, the more stories they have to tell, and often they come at the most unexpected times. This fascinating story was recounted to me by Helen, a work colleague of a family friend. The following story is what she recounted. I agreed to keep the location of the house anonymous, although she was happy for me to say is located in Walton-le-Dale on the outskirts of Preston.

The house used to be the Toll House for a local Hall. The converted bathroom was originally the safe room where they kept money and other valuables from the tolls. Helen said that a builder had looked at it and told her that it didn't look like a safe room, but more like a cell. The walls are 67 centimetres thick (about 2 feet), with concrete and stone floors. The date 1899 is written on one of the beams upstairs, although the house next door is much older.

Helen told me there is a black cat painted on the outside wall which was there before she moved in and nobody knows how long it has been there. She said she had a black cat called Spooky when they first moved in, so this was just another reason to buy it!.

View of the house with the cat on the wall. Photograph taken by the owner. (c) Craig Bryant

There are rifle racks in the hallway and a horse hook on the outside wall so when travellers paid the toll there was somewhere to tie up the horse.

Helen said that 'spooky things' have happened ever since she lived there. When she originally viewed the house with the intent on buying it she said she knew deep down that there was an atmosphere. However, she proceeded to buy the house and moved in during April 2014.

One story Helen recounted was that a friend was sleeping upstairs and she said that during the night someone blew a 'raspberry' in her ear. She said she was woken and it scared her. Later she brought a friend to see the house and this lady said that she could feel the spirit of a small boy, and she said he had a disability of some kind.

When Helen moved in, she had some boxes upstairs on the landing and one day she could hear a remote-control toy car making a whirring sound, like the electric motor was running. When she went up to see what was going on it stopped, but the aerial was moving. She said she found the remote control close by and that nobody else was there.

This happened again when some friends came to stay. They said that in the middle of the night they could hear another electronic toy making noises as if somebody was pushing the buttons, but that nobody else was there.

When her brother came to stay, the door to the tallboy (which is a small wardrobe) opened by itself waking him up. He was shocked to say the least. The interesting part of this, however, is that the door had been jammed for months, and she had decided that the lock must be broke and that they would be unable to open it.

Helen's daughter (who is 8 at the time of writing this) is always asking her if she was calling her name. Her daughter said she can often hear someone saying her name, or that an invisible someone in the room just said her name out loud. When she was about three years old, she pointed towards the washing machine and asked "Why has that little boy not got any legs?" The washing machine is in the kitchen extension which was built around the 1970's or 1980's, prior to her moving in, and given what her daughter saw it is probably right to assume the floor had been raised in the past.

Helen continued that one morning she was carrying her daughter down stairs and she said "Morning!" to her, in a singing sort of voice. Her daughter, laughing as young children do, mimicked her, replying "Morning" in the same singing tone. Suddenly they both heard another voice sing, "Morning" in exactly the same voice that they had. Helen said there was only the two of them in the house at the time and that it sounded like a little boy's voice.

On another occasion, Helen said that she was in bed in the middle of the night and was suddenly woken up by someone poking her in the back. She was alone and terrified. She said she was so terrified she shut her eyes so tightly until the morning and she daren't turn around in bed just in case somebody was there! Another night she was woken up by someone stroking her ear with a cold finger.

Helen concluded her story by saying she believed she had once glimpsed the little boy that seemed to be sharing the house with her and her daughter. One day last summer she was walking from the kitchen to the garage, and as she passed the downstairs bedroom window, she glimpsed a small boy standing at the window. He was dressed in old clothes, staring back at her. Every hair on her head stood up on end and she had an extremely unsettling feeling. She said it frightened the life out of her.

Helen said she often hears whistling down stairs when she is on the first floor or items fall over or randomly drop to the floor. Often, the door knocker bangs but when she goes to see who is there, there is nobody. The knocker is very heavy, and Helen said it had banged of its own accord at least twice in the week prior to her talking to me!

Whoever this little boy is, he is clearly stuck somehow to the house. He is mischievous; although not destructive but he does seem to enjoy frightening guests. The fact that he has no legs is interesting, is it simply that he comes from a time when the floors were lower in the house, or was Helen's guest who said there was a little boy with special needs correct all along?

Did my father see ghosts?

When: 1980's

Source – Author

Was my father psychic and did he see my grandfather on the day of his funeral?

My father sadly passed away in 1998. He was a very straight talking, pragmatic Lancastrian who was not given to making up tall tales. He had a sense of humour, and a kind nature and looking back he perhaps had an ability to see things that only people who have seen ghosts or spirits have.

My father told me two tales which obviously resonated with him, and he didn't seem to be able to explain. I have no doubt that he was being truthful, after all, he was not in the habit of making up tall tales.

The first was a few years after we had moved into a house when I was in my late teens. The house was a semi-detached bungalow built in the 1930's which was joined by two garages. Facing the house, to the right there was a driveway and gate to the rear garden, and an attached garage to the left. The house next door was a mirror image with the garages adjoined in the middle. To walk through the garden a person had to first walk down the driveway, through the gate, past the lounge bay window and round the back of the house to the rear of the garage. The only way out was to climb over a five-foot wall which separated the garden from next door.

The house was unoccupied when my parents bought it, having been owned by an elderly lady who had passed away a few months earlier. My father told me that one afternoon, he was standing in the bay window of the lounge looking at the garden when to his utter shock, an elderly lady moved past the window in full view toward the back of the house and garage. My father said he could see her so clearly, she was wearing a knitted shawl, had her hair piled up in a bun, and wore round steel rimmed glasses that he said were 'perched on the edge of her nose'. Somewhat bewildered, he hurried into the kitchen and opened the back door, expecting to see an elderly woman stood there, but instead he saw no one. He said he quickly went around into the garden and to the front of the house but he saw nothing. Standing at the bottom of the driveway he looked up and down the road, half expecting to see the old lady, but again he saw no one.

My father said he had no logical explanation for what he had seen and said there was no way she could have turned around and disappeared from site so quickly. He said the car was in the garage and the door locked. He checked the garage and then went next door to see if our neighbour could shed any light on the matter, but he had been sat in his chair, in his lounge, overlooking his garden and saw no one go past, so she did not, however unlikely, vault the wall and exit in the direction of next door. My father was, as he put it at the time, 'perplexed' by the whole incident.

Whilst I lived there, I sometimes had an odd feeling that I was not alone, and often saw shadows on the walls, especially in the lounge. On one occasion I thought I saw the outline of a person pressed against the heavy velvet curtains that hung across the bay window.

My father also told me another story which seemed to affect him more, which happened a number of years earlier. It concerned my maternal grandfather, Bill. I remember him telling this story, and that it still shook him up to recall what had happened.

My grandfather always sat in the same chair in the lounge. It was a single chair next to the open coal fire, and it was there that I used to sit with him as a child as he told me ghost stories. Although he gave up smoking in later life, when he smoked he would apparently sit there puffing away on cigarette after cigarette with his feet up toasting them against the coals. My grandmother, Ruby, was a typical no-nonsense Lancashire woman who was born near the start of the 20th century, worked in the cotton mills under appalling conditions and brought up two children during the war whilst Bill served in the RAF in Egypt. Her place was on the three-piece settee.

I spent a lot of my childhood years at their house. My parents both worked long hours and my grandmother would look after me when I was too young to go to school and then as I got older, I would spend my summer holidays there. I remember the Vauxhall Viva that my grandfather had in the 1970's; the exhaust was so loud you could hear him coming two miles away! He used to take us for days out in the car; he loved the Forest of Bowland, an area which is right on the doorstep of where I now live, and Pendle Hill. He loved the coast as well, and often took us for days out to Blackpool or Morecambe. When he died in 1983, I was in my mid teens and I felt a huge loss in my life.

My father recalled the day of his funeral. He was quite close to Bill. As he knew he was passing, Bill asked my father to promise that he would look after my grandmother, which he of course agreed to do. He passed away shortly afterward.

I remember the funeral vividly. It rained during the cremation (it always seemed to rain at funerals) and afterwards we retired back to my grandmother's house for the typical Lancashire 'wake', the gathering after a funeral for family and friends to remember the deceased, eat lots of sandwiches and get a little bit drunk in the process. It was all about 'giving them a good send off'.

At my grandfather's funeral there were a number of people stood in the lounge and the kitchen, a few sat down, but no one sat in his chair. I don't think my Grandmother ever sat in that chair after he died and she didn't like anyone sitting there without permission. My father said that as he was milling around chatting to guests, he walked through the lounge into the kitchen and in doing so, saw out of the corner of his eye someone was sat in my grandfather's chair. My father stopped, looked and said he saw Bill sat there, gazing straight ahead and smiling. A few seconds later he quickly faded away. No one else in the room seemed to notice, they just carried on with the conversations as if nothing had happened.

When my father told this story, I asked if he believed he *had* seen my grandfather that day and he told me that he could not think of any explanation other than it was him. Had he seen an actual ghost, and was my grandfather witness to his own funeral?

Pendle Hill

Source – Various Local legends, Historical Accounts and the Author

The legend of The Pendle Witches and their legacy. A horrifying story of dark acts and a chilling injustice.

Pendle Hill. Photograph taken from Bowland Fell © Craig Bryant

Pendle, old Pendle, thou standest alone

Twixt Burnley and Clitheroe, Whalley and Colne,

Where Hodder and Ribble's fair waters do meet,

With Barley and Downham content at thy feet.

(Anonymous)

No book on Paranormal Lancashire would be complete without a chapter on Pendle Hill. As I write this, on a cold and gloomy early March day, I look out of my window and can see Pendle brooding in the low clouds. There is definitely something magical, and mystical, about it.

The name Pendle comes from the old Cumbric 'Pen' (Cumbric was a local dialect of old English) and old English 'Hyll', both of which mean 'Hill'. In effect, Pendle derives its name from 'Hill Hill'!

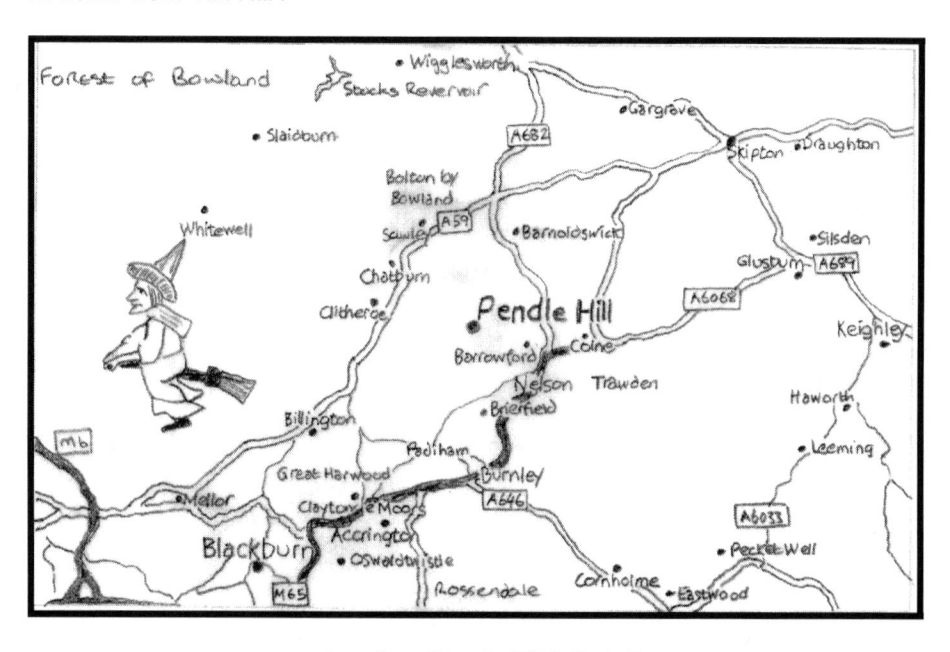

Location of Pendle Hill © Craig Bryant

Standing at 1,827 feet (557 metres), and shaped like half a tear drop on its side, it is detached from the Pennines to the East, the Bowland Fells to the North West and the West Pennine Moors to the South. Although famous for its 17th Century Witch Trials, it is less famous as being the site of Richard Townley's barometer experiments of 1661, and it was atop Pendle Hill that George Fox had a vision in 1652 which led to the foundation of the Quaker Movement.

The 'Shoulder of Pendle'. A different view taken from the eastern end of the hill © Craig Bryant.

Pendle Hill is most famous however for the Witch Trials of 1612. It is now considered one of the great miscarriages of justice in English legal history. The trial centred on two families who lived in the area around Pendle Hill, a local magistrate and several unfortunate local characters.

There are many books on the subject of the Lancashire Witch Trials of 1612, indeed, as I look at my bookshelf, I can see several books on the subject all of which conclude that the trials were an unfortunate and unjust history of the political times. It should be worth noting that in the early 17th century, this part of Lancashire in particular was considered somewhat lawless and 'fabled for its theft, violence and sexual laxity' by the authorities. Things had been made significantly worse since the dissolution of nearby Whalley Abbey in 1537 by Henry VIII, which had exerted a strong religious influence on the predominantly poor peasantry that lived in the area.

When James I (James VI of Scotland) came to the English Throne following the death of Elizabeth I, he was a particularly strong believer in Protestantism and was convinced that there was a plot to remove him by Catholic sympathisers. He was a strong believer in Witchcraft which was exacerbated in 1590 following his attendance at the North Berwick Witch trials in Scotland. The Accused, he believed, were responsible for sending a storm which nearly sank the boat he and his wife Ann were sailing on whilst returning from a trip to Denmark. In 1592 James wrote a book called 'Daemonologie' in which he instructed his followers and fellow Protestants to denounce and prosecute any supporters or practitioners of Witchcraft. James was becoming more obsessed and paranoid by the subject of Witches, and believed they were present at every turn.

A year after ascending to the English throne, a law was enacted imposing the death penalty in cases where it was proven that harm had been caused through the use of magic or corpses had been exhumed for magical purposes. By 1612, he had instructed every 'Justice of the Peace', in effect a local Magistrate, to compile a list of all 'Recusants' – those who refused to attend the Anglican Church or practice Protestantism. Into this toxic atmosphere of accusation and counter accusation stepped Roger Nowell, the Justice of the Peace for Pendle who resided at Read Hall near Burnley. In 1612 he heard a complaint by the family of a pedlar and travelling merchant, John Law, who had allegedly been injured by Witchcraft. Many of those who were to be implicated did indeed consider themselves witches, a description which only later conjured up images of black cats, pointy hats and broomsticks. In the 17th Century, such 'Witches' were no more than wise men and women, skilled in the art of healing using natural remedies often in return for payments, and were accepted as part of rural village life. Sadly, in these dark times, the word 'Witch' began to take on a darker meaning.

The story goes thus. John Law from Halifax had been travelling on horseback when he came upon two local characters – Elizabeth Southerns (known locally as 'Demdike') and her granddaughter, Alizon Device. Demdike was the Matriarch of a well known but poor local family, and had been considered a 'Witch' by her family and peers for over 50 years. They asked Law for some pins. In the 17th Century, metal pins were handmade and quite expensive, and they were believed to be useful for magical purposes, such as healing (particularly for treating warts), divination, and for 'love magic', something which was greatly sought after by some folk! It may have been because of their association with witchcraft that Law was so reluctant to sell them to the two women. Law refused the women's request. Law's son, Abraham, later claimed that Demdike and Device had no intention of paying for the pins and were begging for them instead. Whatever the truth, what happened next would set in motion a series of events that will forever be synonymous with Pendle Hill.

After Law had refused to conduct any transaction with the two women, he was riding away when suddenly, and unfortunately for all parties involved, he suffered a stroke and fell from his horse. He managed to get to his feet and stagger to a nearby Inn. Initially he made no accusations against Alizon, who seemed to be the main protagonist in the incident. However, she seemed convinced by her own powers and, perhaps enjoying the attention, confessed she had injured Law by foul means and asked for forgiveness.

Alizon Device, her mother Elizabeth, and her brother James were summoned to appear before Nowell on 30 March 1612. Alizon confessed that she had sold her soul to the Devil, and that she had asked Lucifer to lame John Law after he had refused to give her some pins. Her brother, James, stated that his sister had also confessed to bewitching a local child. Elizabeth was more reticent, admitting only that her mother, Demdike, had a mark on her body, something that many, including Nowell, would have regarded as proof that the Devil had sucked her blood in return for favours. It was believed that he often manifested himself as an animal such as a goat, a dog or a black cat. When questioned about Anne Whittle (known locally as Old Chattox), the matriarch of the other family reputedly involved in witchcraft in and around Pendle, Alizon perhaps saw this as an opportunity for revenge. There had been bad blood between the two families, possibly dating back to 1601, when a member of Chattox's family broke into Malkin Tower, the home of the Devices, and stole goods worth about £1 (equivalent to about £117 as of today). It was also reported that there were disagreements over where each family would beg, as there were more lucrative spots along the roads and near to Inns where more people would gather.

Alizon accused Chattox of murdering four men by witchcraft, and of killing her father, John Device, who had died in 1601. Chattox, by this time, was old, bent and nearly blind, continually muttering away to herself in a low, inaudible chatter (hence the nickname 'Chattox') which many thought was a sign of evil or madness. Alizon claimed that her father had been so frightened of Chattox that he had agreed to give her 8 LBS of oatmeal each year in return for her promise not to hurt his family. The oatmeal was handed over annually until the year before John's death. On his deathbed John claimed that his sickness had been caused by Chattox because they had not paid for her protection the previous year as agreed.

On 2 April 1612, Demdike, Chattox, and Chattox's daughter Anne Redferne, were summoned to appear before Nowell. Both Demdike and Chattox provided Nowell with damning confessions. Demdike claimed that she had given her soul to the Devil 20 years previously, and Chattox said that she had given her soul to "a 'Thing' like a

Christian Man", on his promise that "she would not lack anything and would get any revenge she desired". Although Anne Redferne made no confession, Demdike said that she had seen her making clay figures. These were often made in the likeness of someone they wished to hurt, and would either stick pins in the parts they wished to afflict, or if a more permanent end was required, they could be crumbled and thrown into the fire. They believed this would cause the death of their intended victim.

Margaret Crooke, another witness seen by Nowell that day, claimed that her brother had fallen sick and died after having had a disagreement with Redferne, and that he had frequently blamed her for his illness. Based on the evidence and confessions he had obtained, Nowell committed Demdike, Chattox, Anne Redferne and Alizon Device to Lancaster Gaol, to be tried for 'Maleficium' (causing harm by Witchcraft) at the next Assizes (trial).

The committal and subsequent trial of the four women might have been the end of the matter, had it not been for a meeting organised by Elizabeth Device at Malkin Tower, the home of the Demdikes, held on Good Friday 10 April 1612. Friends and others sympathetic to the family attended, and when word of it reached Roger Nowell, he decided to investigate. On 27 April 1612, an inquiry was held before Nowell and another magistrate, Nicholas Bannister, to determine the purpose of the meeting at Malkin Tower, who had attended, and what had happened there. As a result of the inquiry, eight more people were accused of witchcraft and committed for trial: Elizabeth Device, James Device, Alice Nutter, Katherine Hewitt, John Bulcock, Jane Bulcock, Alice Grey and Jennet Preston. It was guilt by association. Preston lived in Gisburn, then across the border in Yorkshire, so she was sent for trial at York Assizes. The others were sent to Lancaster Gaol, to join the four already imprisoned there.

Some believe that Malkin Tower was situated near the village of Newchurch in Pendle. There is a grave in the graveyard reputedly of Alice Nutter, but in reality, it is the final resting place of two other people named Nutter. Another possible location for Malkin Tower is in the village of Blacko on the site of present-day Malkin Tower Farm. In 2011 workmen found the remains of a 17th century cottage at Lower Black Moss Reservoir near the village of Barley, which nestles against the foot of Pendle Hill. As 2011 was approaching, and the 400th anniversary of the with trials, the media soon latched on to this find and much to their delight the skeleton of a cat was discovered along with numerous artefacts from the 16th and 17th Centuries. Although there is no definitive evidence that this cottage was occupied by any of the Pendle Witches, or that it is the site of the original Malkin Tower, locals soon began to speculate that this did indeed have links with the Witches, perhaps to perpetuate the myths a little more. Certainly, it will have done no harm to local businesses that thrive on 'Witch Tourism'.

The Pendle witches were tried in a group that also included the Samlesbury Witches. These were Jane Southworth, Jennet Brierley, and Ellen Brierley. The charges against them included child murder and cannibalism. Also, on trial was Margaret Pearson, the so-called 'Padiham Witch', who was facing her third trial for witchcraft, this time for killing a horse. Finally, they were accompanied by Isobel Robey from

Windle near St Helens, who was accused of using witchcraft to cause sickness. Some of the accused, such as Alizon Device, seem to have genuinely believed in their guilt, but others protested their innocence to the end. It has been speculated that a lack of education and even a basic understanding of the dire situation they were in led to those who believed they were witches confessing their guilt. It has also been speculated that coming from poor families, probably living in squalid conditions, to suddenly be thrust into the limelight and the subject of such interest was also too intoxicating for these people to ignore, and the attention they received, probably for the first time in their lives, simply led them to perpetuate the accusations levelled at them.

Jennet Preston was tried at York Assizes on 27th July 1612. She was accused of killing Thomas Lister of Westby Hall, and found guilty of Witchcraft. Jennet was hanged on 29th July at Knavesmere, the site of the current York Racecourse.

On 18th August 1612 the trial began of the Pendle Witches. Chattox was accused of the murder of Robert Nutter. She pleaded not guilty, but the confession she had made to Roger Nowell was read out in court, and evidence against her was presented by James Robinson, who had lived with the Chattox family 20 years earlier. He claimed to remember that Nutter had accused Chattox of turning his beer sour, and that she was commonly believed to be a witch. Chattox broke down and admitted her guilt, calling on God for forgiveness and the judges to be merciful to her daughter, Anne Redferne.

Demdike confessed to witchcraft, stating that she had a Familiar called 'Tibb' who came to her in the shape of a black dog. She also claimed that a brown dog had come to her and sucked blood from under her arm.

Elizabeth Device was charged with the murders of James Robinson, John Robinson and, together with Alice Nutter and Demdike, the murder of Henry Mitton. Elizabeth Device vehemently maintained her innocence. Contemporary records state that 'this odious Witch' suffered from a facial deformity resulting in her left eye being set lower than her right. In those dark times, maybe this was enough to convince Nowell that Elizabeth was a Witch. The main witness against Elizabeth was her daughter, Jennet, who was about nine years old. Jennet was brought into the courtroom and asked to stand up and give evidence against her mother. Elizabeth, finding herself confronted with her own child making accusations that could lead to her execution, began to curse and scream at her daughter, forcing the judges to have her removed from the courtroom before the evidence could be heard. Jennet was placed on a table and stated that she believed her mother had been a witch for three or four years. She also said her mother had a Familiar called Ball, who appeared in the shape of a brown dog. Jennet claimed to have witnessed conversations between Ball and her mother, and that Ball had been asked to help with various murders. James Device also gave evidence against his mother, saying he had seen her making a clay figure of one of her victims, John Robinson. Unsurprisingly, Elizabeth Device was found guilty. The question remains, why would the children give such damning evidence against their mother? Were they threatened, coerced or simply not intelligent enough to understand the gravity of their accusation? Was this another case of them simply enjoying being the centre of attention?

James Device pleaded not guilty to the murders by witchcraft of Anne Townley and John Duckworth. However he, like Chattox, had earlier made a confession to Nowell, which was read out in court. That, and the evidence presented against him by his sister Jennet, who said that she had seen her brother asking a black dog he had conjured up to help him kill Townley, was sufficient to persuade the jury to find him guilty as well.

On 19th August, the trials of the three Samlesbury Witches were heard. Anne Redferne made her first appearance in court in the afternoon, charged with the murder of Robert Nutter. The evidence against her was considered unsatisfactory, and she was acquitted.

However, Anne Redferne was not so fortunate the following day, when she faced her second trial, for the murder of Robert Nutter's father, Christopher. She pleaded not guilty to this accusation. Unfortunately, Demdike's statement to Nowell, which accused Anne of having made clay figures of the Nutter family, was read out in court and other witnesses were called to testify that Anne was a witch. Anne refused to admit her guilt to the end. She had given no evidence against any of the other accused, but despite her protestations, she was also found guilty.

Jane Bulcock and her son John Bulcock, both from Newchurch in Pendle, were accused and found guilty of the murder by witchcraft of Jennet Deane. Both denied that they had attended the meeting at Malkin Tower, but Jennet Device identified Jane as having been one of those present, and John as having turned the spit to roast the sheep which had been stolen from a neighbouring farm in order to feed those who attended.

Statue of Alice Nutter at Roughlee, near Pendle Hill © Craig Bryant

Alice Nutter was unusual among the accused in that she was comparatively wealthy as the widow of a tenant yeoman farmer, living at Roughlee Hall. She made no statement either before or during her trial, except to enter her plea of not guilty to the charge of murdering Henry Mitton by witchcraft. The prosecution alleged that she, along with Demdike and Elizabeth Device, had caused Mitton's death after he had refused to give Demdike a penny. The only evidence against Alice seems to have been that James Device claimed Demdike had told him of the murder, and Jennet Device in her statement said that Alice had been present at the Malkin Tower meeting. Alice may have called in on the meeting at Malkin Tower on her way to a secret (and illegal) Good Friday Catholic service, and refused to speak for fear of incriminating her fellow Catholics. Many of the Nutter family were Catholics, and two had been executed as Jesuit priests - John Nutter in 1584 and his brother Robert in 1600. Due to the lack of evidence offered to the contrary, Alice Nutter was found guilty.

Close up of statue of Alice Nutter © Craig Bryant

Katherine Hewitt, also known locally as 'Mould-Heeles', was charged and found guilty of the murder of Anne Foulds, the wife of a clothier from Colne, near Burnley. It was claimed she had attended the meeting at Malkin Tower with Alice Grey. According to the evidence given by James Device, both Hewitt and Grey told the others at that meeting that they had killed Anne Foulds. Jennet Device also claimed Katherine had attended the Malkin Tower meeting.

Alice Grey was also accused of the murder of Anne Foulds. Contemporary records do not provide an account of Alice Grey's trial, simply recording her as one of the Samlesbury witches.

Alizon Device, whose encounter with John Law had triggered the events leading up to the trials, was charged with causing harm by witchcraft. Alizon was confronted in court by her alleged victim, John Law. She seems to have genuinely believed in her own guilt, falling to her knees in tears and confessing her crimes. Unsurprisingly, she too was found guilty.

Under the 1604 Witchcraft Act, Magistrate Bromley had little choice but to pass the sentence of death on those that had been found guilty. On 20th August 1612 the convicted were all taken to the moors above Lancaster and hanged. No 'Witch' was ever burned at the stake in England. Demdike was spared strangulation. She had died whilst in captivity due to the shockingly bad conditions the accused were kept in, and her advanced age and infirmities.

There are no eye witness accounts of the executions. It is likely the condemned were first led up to the gallows above Lancaster, surrounded by a baying crowd of on lookers. At this time in history, public executions were still somewhat of a spectacle and crowds were encouraged to gather to witness the often-gruesome death of the victims as a warning to others who may wish to subvert law and order. The gallows were often made of several long beams with two or three ropes hanging from each beam. At Tyburn in London, the beams were often constructed in a triangle, three at a time, so that multiple executions could take place. The condemned stood on a bench or cart and once the noose was placed around their necks, their support was removed and death was by slow strangulation, rather than breaking the neck. In later times the 'drop method' was employed as a more humane method of dispatch. What became of the bodies is unsure, but it is likely they were burned close by and not returned to Pendle as in some stories.

What we do know is that Little Jennet Device returned to Pendle, although who she lived with is uncertain. We know she returned because some years later she would find herself once again in a court of law, this time as an accused Witch herself.

What led to the confessions of the people involved we will never know. Perhaps they genuinely believed that they were practicing witches, or had seen things that perhaps in reality were more innocent than claimed. Certainly, the incident which started the whole series of events was unfortunate, but the confessions, accusations and counter accusations which followed suggest a feud between two families which soon enveloped a community, and encapsulated those further afield. In a time when anyone not openly practicing the Anglican faith, and perhaps still clinging to old pagan rituals and traditional medicines, were viewed with suspicion by the Authorities, it is perhaps unsurprising that this case escalated as quickly as it did. No doubt the Judge and Jury had some preconceptions of the accused and some of the confessions may have been forced or simply made up. Whatever the reasons behind the events of 1612, the story of the Lancashire Witches is indelibly linked with Pendle Hill and the surrounding area. Villages that nestle at the foot of Pendle such as Barley, Roughlee, Downham and Newchurch-In-Pendle will always be associated with those dark times and from a personal perspective, I can feel an atmosphere and link with the past that is hard to dismiss. Certainly, local businesses know how to play on the legend that seems to perpetuate from every stone and every inch of moorland across Pendle Hill and use it to their advantage. The area is a magnet for walkers and tourists from all over the world, keen to soak up the unique atmosphere this part of the world has to offer.

Returning to the trials themselves, it is worth noting that there is only one contemporary record of the trials, that written by Thomas Potts, clerk to the Lancashire Assizes at the time of the trial. He was instructed to write an account by the trial judges, and when it was submitted to Bromley he decided that it should be published under the title *'The Wonderfull Discoverie of Witches'* and although it was not a record of what was actually said at the trial, it is a record (however accurate) of what actually happened. It is interesting that the trials took place only 7 years after the Gunpowder Plot and the trial of Guy Fawkes and his cohorts, and that James Device apparently confessed to being part of a plot to blow up Lancaster Gaol with gunpowder in a similar fashion. As preposterous as it sounds, it is perhaps indicative of the times and the willingness of many of the accused to confess to almost anything, no matter how outlandish. It is also worth noting that Potts dedicated his book to Thomas Knyvet and his wife. Knyvet was the man credited with discovering and arresting Guy Fawkes.

In 1633 Jennet Device found herself once again in a court, this time she was accused of witchcraft herself. The 1612 trials could be excused due to the fervour and religious zeal of James I and his followers, but this trial seems to have hinged on nothing more than the Magistrates stirring up another witch hunt. The account is startling in that it shows just how haphazardly the trials were conducted and the callous manner in which the prisoners were treated and shown off no better than animals in a zoo.

Once again, the main source of evidence was offered and accepted by a child, a boy of eleven named Edward Robinson. Edward resided at Wheatley Lane and had been out on the evening of November 1st 1633 looking for Bulloes – wild plums – when he said he saw two greyhounds approach him. One was black and the other brown. Each dog had a string around its neck and as he grabbed them, he saw a hare rise up close by and bolt into the hedgerow. To his surprise, neither dog gave chase and in a fit of anger the boy started to beat each dog with a 'twich', or stick, that he was carrying. All of a sudden, one of the greyhounds reared up and turned into 'Dickinson's wife' whom he knew and the other turned into a boy, whom he didn't recognise. Dickinson's Wife offered him a shilling (an enormous sum of money in those days) if he would keep quiet about what he saw. Robinson declined and made it abundantly clear he would denounce her as a witch. She took a bridle from her clothes and put it on the boy (who had now turned into a white horse) and forced Robinson to ride back to a house called Hoarestones (also on Wheatley Lane). Robinson stated that he saw a group of men and women gathered there, feasting. He said he saw one woman take three clay pictures down from a beam in the ceiling and stick them full of thorns. Managing to escape without much trouble, although he said he was followed by two witches as far as' Boggart Hole' (Boggart is a local word for a mischievous spirit – see later chapter), he was soon found by his father also named Edmund Robinson. Edmund senior was described as a poor man, whose profession was that of a 'Waller' or Mason. Young Edmund was encouraged to recount his tale to the local Magistrates. It was not until three months later that the evidence was taken down at Padiham, near to Pendle Hill itself. The Magistrates were Richard Shuttleworth of Gawthorpe and John Starkie of Huntroyd. As a consequence of young Robinson's testimony, a number of suspects were rounded up, taken to Lancaster and tried. Seventeen were found guilty. Even by 17th century judicial standards, the trial was a shambles, with accounts recording that one of the accused complained she could not be heard giving evidence over the shouts and screams of the baying crowd that had crammed into the court and surrounding area. However, instead of being taken the next day to the place of execution and hanged, a report was sent to Charles I and his privy council in London. In turn, they instructed one Henry Bridgeman, Bishop of Chester, to examine some of the women. Before he could conclude his findings however, four of the women were taken from Lancaster to London and lodged at the Ship Tavern in Greenwich, near one of the Royal residences. They were in turn examined by various surgeons, midwives and even Charles himself. William Harvey, famous for demonstrating the circulation of blood, wrote that he '*inspected the bodies of Jennet Hargreaves, Frances Dickinson and Mary Spencer...and found no marks or teats or anything unnatural*'. One can only imagine how degrading this must have been for the subjects.

However, attitudes were changing and during the reign of Charles I there were only six documented executions for witchcraft. The fate of those who had stood trial is somewhat uncertain, however it is recorded that at least some of them were still resident in Lancaster Gaol three years later. In the accounts of the trial, an interesting fact is mentioned. Jennet Device had a half-brother, William, something which is not mentioned in the original trial transcripts from 1612. Nothing is known of him, or his parentage.

After the trials, young Edward Robinson was set up as a witch-finder by his father and uncle, touring Sunday services in churches in the locality where he proceeded to detect witches. Just how, short of blackmail, they were able to turn young Robinson's act into a profit is unclear, but it is known that his previously poor father suddenly had the wealth to buy two cows. However, their reign was short, the boy and his father and uncle were summoned to London where they were separated. Young Robinson confessed he had made up his original story and that his father had encouraged him to continue after the trial. We do not know what happened to the men, but young Edmund Robinson returned to his village of birth and slipped into the mists of history.

Today, there are no hoards of ghosts rampaging over Pendle Hill every night, and there are certainly no covens of witches active as far as I know. An image has slipped into the psyche of many a paranormal tourist or excited child who visits Pendle Hill, one of an old crone, resplendent with pointy had, broomstick, ubiquitous black cat and cauldron, bent over almost double cackling away as she makes yet another potion designed to hurt or maim her next unsuspecting victim. 'Eye of Newt' indeed!

Plaque which accompanies statue of Alice Nutter © Craig Bryant

There may be a link between the Paranormal and Unidentified Flying Objects in the Pendle area, and perhaps there is a correlation between the two which have perpetuated the myth of Witches roaming over Pendle for the last 400 years.

The area around Pendle Hill, North towards Caton Moor near Skipton, East towards Todmorden and Hebden Bridge and South towards the Rossendale Valley have long been associated with UFO sightings. Indeed, as recently as 2015, Lancashire Police received a number of calls from members of the public who had seen 'flashing lights like disco balls' hovering around 3,000 feet above Pendle Hill. The Ministry of Defence also released files in 2008 which catalogue a number of UFO sightings in the area of Pendle Hill. The most famous sighting in the area is the Hebden Bridge UFO case, in which PC Alan Godfrey claims to have witnessed a UFO in November of 1980 and 'lost' a significant amount of time, unable to remember what happened to him for at least 2 hours. In 2009 reports were made to Lancashire Police of numerous objects above Haslingen and Helmshore in the Rossendale Valley which were bright, colourful and flew in a triangular formation. In 1979 reports came in to Police in Blackburn of a bright object hovering over the Royal Ordnance Factory in Darwen. The investigating officers who arrived to witness the object even drew pictures of what they saw, which looked remarkably like flying 'saucers'.

As recently as 11th December 2018, I witnessed first hand a bright light in the sky over Pendle Hill, which behaved like no aircraft, satellite or shooting star I had ever seen. It was early, around 6-30pm, and a perfectly clear, crisp winter's evening. Travelling quickly from east to west, the bright light (almost like a star) suddenly stopped, made several tight clockwise circles, turned sharply at right angles and moved at speed in a southerly direction. It then made a sharp right-angled turn back westward before suddenly disappearing. Interestingly, reports in the press the following day confirmed that something had been tracked by radar and that RAF fighter jets had been scrambled to intercept an object south of their base in Lossiemouth, Scotland. Unlike most incidents such as this, where it later transpires that the object was a Russian military aircraft that had somehow strayed into British airspace, no such follow up reports were made about this sighting.

So, what is the correlation between the Pendle Witches and UFO's over Pendle Hill? Over the years, myths have grown up around witchcraft, that all witches wear pointy hats, have black cats, and fly on broomsticks. It may be that over the years Pendle Hill has been host to many strange lights in the sky; no doubt many could be called UFO's. These days, many so called UFO's are explained away as aircraft or stellar phenomenon, but go back a few hundred years before manned flight was even thought about, how do you explain away bright lights in the sky over Pendle Hill? Local people could only have put them down to witches or ghostly demons flying through the air on their broomsticks, cackling as they went, wreaking havoc in the sleepy towns and villages that lie around Pendle and beyond. Perhaps the sightings of UFO's over the years have simply served to strengthen the myth of witches and ghosts still habiting Pendle Hill to this day.

Whether it be legends of witchcraft, or strange lights in the sky, Pendle Hill certainly has its own unique atmosphere of the paranormal and strangeness. To walk up the 'Shoulder' of Pendle on a bright clear day and stand on the summit taking in the spectacular 360-degree views is one of life's truly wonderful moments. I feel very lucky to live in the shadow of one of Northern Britain's iconic, natural wonders.

Proof of an Afterlife?

When – 1998

Source – Author and Family Member

How did the Medium know so much about my family, and my recent loss?

Do they really have contact with the deceased? After reading these stories, you might well think so……

Despite my scepticism towards mediums and those who claim to be able to speak to the dead, I am including this story because it raises a number of questions. Can mediums really converse with the dead, or are they just clever frauds that research and glean information from the grieving and desperate in order to tell them just what they want to hear? Even before the days of the Internet, a name or an address could easily lead someone to discover a recently deceased relative through obituary columns in the local newspapers. From that, a picture of that persons life could easily be pieced together, often including family names, spouse, work career and so on. From that information, it would be easy to convince a grieving widow or family member that they are in spiritual contact with a loved one, telling them things they 'shouldn't' know about the deceased. Perhaps I'm being too harsh. Perhaps giving someone hope that their loved ones are safe and happy 'on the other side' isn't perhaps such a bad thing. Perhaps they are simply offering a service that some are happy to pay for.

A number of years ago I was persuaded by a female work colleague to pay a visit to a well-known medium in Preston, the town where I was working at the time. The gentleman in question had the ubiquitous crystal ball and all manner of mystical objects adorning his front room. He was of African descent, and adorned the room with paraphernalia associated with Black Magic and the Dark Arts; Skulls, Tarot Cards and creepy looking dolls.

I sat in a chair opposite him as he gazed into his crystal ball. He immediately told me that I had recently lost my dad to a long illness, and that he was watching over me along with another 'spirit' who he could not identify. I do recall him telling me it was female. He also said that the lady I was in a relationship with at the time would not last, and that I would not marry her. He was right!

I left feeling somewhat disturbed. I knew that my work colleague had only given the Medium our first names and no other information. If he was a Charlatan, then how could he possibly have discovered that my father had recently passed away just from the name 'Craig'. Bear in mind that I lived 20 miles or so from Preston anyway, so my father's obituary some 6 months earlier had not been in the local Preston newspaper. That left the perplexing possibility that he could indeed see things I couldn't, and that my father and this other 'spirit' were actually with me. It left me wondering whether some people could see the deceased and mentally converse with them, in a similar way to some people being able to see or sense ghosts, just on a different 'frequency'.

A similar experience happened to my mother; again, this was about 6 months after my father had died. My mother has never been a particularly spiritual person, although her family were descended from Irish Catholics and some of that religious zeal had been passed down from the first Irish immigrants to land in Liverpool some three generations earlier. After my father died, she rediscovered religion and started attending church every Sunday. When my father was alive, he had two neighbours who he was particularly friendly with. Alan had lived across the road and sadly passed away a couple of months after my father. It was his widow who convinced my mother they should both visit a medium.

As with my experience, my Mother swore that both her and her neighbour had only given their first names. She said they gave no hint of an address or any other details. Now, it is entirely possible that the information this Medium had found out was through painstaking research in the local newspaper, looking back through months (if not years) of obituaries to try to match my Mother and her Friend to death notices. It is, of course, possible that she *was* in contact with 'the other side' and that what she told my Mother was entirely true. According to my mother, the medium sat her down and immediately looked straight at her, telling her that Dave was fine (David was my father's first name, but only close family or friends called him 'Dave') and that he and Alan were fine and having a whale of a time 'on the other side'!

So, the question remains – are mediums frauds or do they really have the ability to converse with the deceased? If they are, then are these stories proof of an afterlife?

Unit Four Cinema – Accrington

Source – Various

When – From 1930's onwards

A tall, thin shadowy man haunts the stalls and a cinema cat called Lucifer! The ghost of this old, atmospheric cinema has been seen for nearly 70 years.

Accrington cinema with The Shifters bar to the left. Photograph unknown.

Like most northern towns, Accrington has had its fair share of economic ups and downs. The town was built on Cotton. When I was a boy Howard and Bullough's, which was later bought by Platt Saco Lowell, employed hundreds of local people making weaving looms for the cotton industry. As I grew up in the 70's and 80's this industry was in terminal decline, and had been for a few decades previously, unable to compete with cheap imports of cotton from the Far East and India.

The town centre suffered greatly from economic decline and successive councils tried to reinvigorate the town by demolishing old buildings in favour of new, airy and light shopping units. I remember when the new Arndale Centre was built on the site of a huge municipal car park right in the centre of town and the demolition of some fascinating old buildings adjacent to make way for new shops. On the site of the Shifters Public Bar and Unit Four Cinema now stands a Boots the Chemist and an O2 mobile phone shop. I spent many of my formative years in The Shifters, a three floored disco-cum-nightclub formally called 'The Pickwick' in the 1970's which had rather a rough reputation. I wasn't the only one who shed a little tear when The Shifters was raised to the ground. Sadly, the magnificent cinema next door was also demolished, leaving Accrington, like many towns of it day, without somewhere to watch the latest blockbusters. I fondly remember my father taking me to see Star Wars there in 1977, and I have vague memories of a James Bond double bill one Saturday afternoon – Goldfinger and Dr No. I also remember seeing a Doug McClure film there with some rather unconvincing dinosaurs, the special effects were bad, even in the pre computerised days of stop-motion animation.

Delving into the history of the cinema, I found that in 1950 Accrington had six cinemas in the town centre in total, with another eight in the neighbouring towns of Oswaldtwistle, Church, Clayton-Le-Moors, Rishton and Great Harwood. Accrington's cinemas had dwindled to just two in 1960. As a very young child I remember another cinema called 'The Prince's' (I may be wrong on the name as my memory is somewhat foggy on this one) which was on a side road, off Blackburn Road, near to the railway bridge. This cinema was nicknamed 'The Flea Pit' and closed sometime in the early 1970's.

That left just the Unit Four (as it became known in 1973 after a refurbishment), and its less than salubrious drinking establishment next door. Interestingly, both buildings were built on three floors and the third floors were connected by a stockroom which, in The Shifters, was behind the 3rd floor bar, and in the cinema somewhere behind the giant screen in one of the auditoriums. The cinema had a particular feel to it, it may have been the burgundy velour seats and the 1930's décor or just the fact it was dark most of the time, and smelt a bit musty and old. My late father used to go to watch the Saturday Matinees there as a boy in the late 1940's and 1950's. He told me he remembered being so excited every Saturday morning for the next instalment of Flash Gordon (in black and white of course) and that he and his friends always used to say that the cinema was haunted. None of them would sit at the back because of the ghost that reputedly had been seen on numerous occasion gliding around the back of the stalls. Growing up, I heard the same story from a number of sources. The figure was allegedly that of a man, tall and thin and although often dark and shadowy, it was occasionally luminescent enough to be seen standing at the back of the Stalls with the lights down. On more than one occasion it had been mistaken for the usherette with her torch, who used to guide people to empty seats when the film had started. Some said he wore a top hat and a cloak (very dramatic!), some said he was dressed as a manual worker from the post war years (this will become significant later) and some said he was just a tall, dark man. The story seemed to be somewhat steeped in urban myth and was perhaps a construct of numerous stories all rolled into one, but whatever his appearance or purpose, there was no doubt that something haunted the old cinema.

An acquaintance of mine told me of an unnerving incident when he was briefly working behind the bar in The Shifters. He left shortly afterwards, vowing never to work there again and seemed genuinely shaken by the whole episode. He told me that one evening he had been assigned to the third-floor bar, and was tidying up after the premises had shut and was alone, loading the dishwasher with glasses and wiping down the bar. He went into the stockroom behind the bar and as he was deliberating which crates needed replenishing, he became aware he was not alone. He said, and this was coming from a very sceptical person who I had known for years, that a figure suddenly floated through the far wall from the Cinema on the other side and passed close by to where he was standing, disappearing through the wall into the public bar behind him. Although extremely startled he said he put his head around the door to see if the figure was in the bar, but he saw nothing. Somewhat shaken, he described the figure as that of a man, tall, thin and gaunt, recalling the features on his face with great clarity. He said it was only the torso, no legs, and floated through the storeroom preceded by a cold draft. After the incident he decided he did not want to work there any more and although still sceptical as to the existence of ghosts, he could not explain in rational terms what it was he had seen.

Having done some further research whilst writing this book, it would seem that the Ghost in this case has been rather busy over the years. The story goes back to 1974 and a report in the Manchester Evening News newspaper. When the cinema was being converted into three screens apparently all sorts of supernatural phenomena were witnessed. As soon as the conversion work began the cinema and workers were plagued by supernatural occurrences.

The cinema was still open to the public despite the renovation work, and the first instance of anything strange was during the midnight showing of an 'X' rated film. The curtains closed of their own accord half way through the 'performance', witnessed by a good many disgruntled patrons!

The Cinema Manager at the time was a gentleman by the name of Sidney Gournelle. One night he reputedly saw a blue light hovering in mid air in a corridor and when he approached, shining his torch in the direction of the light, it cast a shadow of a tall thin man on the door behind.

A workman was walking down the same corridor when he felt two icy hands gripping his shoulders. He apparently ran for his life and never returned to the cinema.

When Mr Gournelle tried to force Lucifer, the cinema cat, (yes, really, I had to read that twice as well!) into the projection room, it flew down the stairs and, apparently panic stricken, clawed an usherette!

A local medium was brought in and described the events as those of an irate ghost. The Medium continued the spirit was that of a workman killed in an accident on the site when the original cinema was being built back in the 1930's. The spirit, according to the medium, was expressing his disapproval of the building work in the cinema. Apparently, he didn't like the renovations!

Things got so bad that a priest was called in to exorcise the cinema. Although the newspaper stated that the priest wished to remain anonymous, contemporary reports suggest that the paranormal activity subsided after the exorcism, although there was still a noticeable chill in the cinema even on hot summer days. Quite obviously the exorcism only quietened the ghost for a while and various manifestations started up again shortly afterwards.

The story of the Unit Four cinema ghost has probably been long forgotten, as has the building itself. It is over 20 years since the cinema and adjacent nightclub were demolished and I occasionally wonder if anyone working in the shops that replaced them has ever witnessed or felt anything strange. If indeed it was the ghost of a deceased worker from the 1930's, maybe he was trapped in the fabric of the building and once demolished he was released and able to move on. If anyone knows different, I'd like to hear more!

The Fisherman's Cottage, Staithes, North Yorkshire

Source – Author

When – 2001

Old Victorian photographs that follow you around the room, a dark atmosphere and a nocturnal manifestation during a storm......

Although this incident did not happen within the County of Lancashire, it is so remarkable that I felt I had to include it in this book.

Staithes is a pretty little coastal village on the North Yorkshire coast, a few miles north of Whitby. The area has a reputation for paranormality and unexplained sightings of UFO's as well as unexplained animal carcasses that have been found mutilated. Staithes nestles on the coast with the imposing North Yorkshire moors behind it. A drive across the moors in any weather is an experience, as it rises to well over 1000 feet above sea level and is a barren, windswept plateau.

A number of years ago I rented a cottage in Staithes for the weekend. I had never visited the village before and love the North Yorkshire coastline, having visited Whitby and Scarborough on a few occasions. As I drove down into the village, I was struck by how picturesque it was, with its tiny harbour and colourful little fishing boats bobbing up and down gently on the sea. It looked picture perfect, with the sun glinting off the sea and seagulls circling and crying overhead. Little did I know that my weekend get away was about to take a rather paranormal twist!

Arriving at the cottage, I immediately felt a feeling of unease as I opened the door and walked into the hallway. It was a very old cottage, probability 17th century, maybe older. The floors were uneven, the whitewashed walls were adorned with black and white photos of Victorian fishing families that seemed to leer from the picture frames and follow me wherever I went. It made me feel very uncomfortable. The scenes were of fishermen and women, hard, grizzled individuals, moulded by the sea and the bleakness of their existence. The men were all gnarled, with huge beards and smoking pipes whilst the women glared at the camera with a hard resolve. Fishing nets hung up behind them, and unwashed children sat by their feet. There was not the glimmer of a smile between them.

Although it was late summer outside, the inside of the cottage felt freezing cold. The main downstairs room was very pretty, with small mullioned windows overlooking the village and the sea beyond, oak beams and an open fire. On the mantelpiece I remember an old carriage clock which ticked loudly and somewhat menacingly in a monotonous rhythm. It seemed to get louder and louder the more I stared at it. There were more of the horrible photographs on the walls and these seemed to follow me even more intently than the ones in the entrance hall. I had the distinct feeling that I was not alone and it was very unnerving.

I have made up, and successfully lit, any number of open fires and wood burners in my time. I looked at the fire place and decided to build a fire, a bit of warmth would cheer the place up! However, no matter what I did I could not get the fire to take hold. It may have been that the chimney needed a good brushing, but there was absolutely no draw on the fire at all and the wisps of smoke that I managed to coax from the kindling just drifted into my face rather than up the chimney. Eventually I gave up. There was no way the fire was going to light.

The next moment all the lights went out. It was twilight outside and the small windows in the cottage did not let in much light. Suddenly, to add to the cold and the feeling of being watched I was suddenly plunged into semi darkness. At that moment I came to the conclusion someone, or something, did not want me in the house.

Scrabbling around in the semi darkness I finally found the dilapidated fuse box and, despite a real fear of electrocuting myself, I found the offending blown fuse and replaced it. Thankfully there was box of spares next to the box. At this point I decided to walk down to the pub on the harbour and have some food and a drink or two to steady my nerves. My idyllic weekend away was becoming less idyllic as the minutes ticked by, just like the diabolical clock on the mantelpiece.

I decided to take a walk down the hill to the harbour and the public house which overlooked it. I had a lovely meal and a couple of drinks and feeling somewhat fortified I decided it was time to return to the 'Haunted Cottage' as I had now renamed it, and put the early evening incidents down to bad luck and an over excitable imagination. Little did I know.

As I opened the front door, I held my breath and flicked the light switch, half expecting nothing to happen. By now it was dark outside and the cottage had been plunged into pitch black. I breathed a huge sigh of relief as the lights flickered on – and I do mean flickered – for a moment I thought the mains box was about to fuse again. Thankfully it didn't.

I attempted to light the fire again. After much cursing I gave up and sat heavily in an old wing backed armchair. I looked around the room, and the photographs glared back. The clock ticked louder and louder..........

I decided it was time for bed. I walked up the narrow, steep, creaking stairs and as I reached the top, I again had that feeling of dread. It is difficult to explain but I felt that there was another person in the cottage and that I was an unwanted visitor. I concluded that whoever had lived there before had not left, and did not want me in the cottage.

I got ready for bed and climbed in, pulling the heavy duvet up to my chin and lay there like some frightened child furtively looking around the room, seeing shadows move in every corner and hearing creaks and knocks every few seconds. I was still trying to convince myself that it was all in my imagination and that a combination of creepy photographs and bad luck with the fire and the lights had heightened my senses to fever pitch. I shifted about uncomfortably in the bed. The mattress was horrid, lumpy and uncomfortable with springs sticking in my back and legs.

I must have drifted off because suddenly I was woken with a start and sat bolt upright in bed. My heart was pumping so fast I thought it was going to burst out of my chest. The room was dark and all I could hear was the howling of the wind and lashing of the rain outside as it battered the windows of the bedroom. A North Sea storm had blown in without warning and was lashing the coastline with spine chilling ferocity. The bedroom door suddenly swung open, despite there being a sturdy iron latch on the inside, and this made me jump so much that I reached over to turn the bedside lamp on and see what had just happened. I told myself I hadn't closed the door properly and that it was just the wind. After all, the whole cottage seemed to be creaking and groaning in time with the storm that was now reaching full force outside.

Then, from nowhere, I felt I was not alone. I looked towards the door and saw a dark mass move across the bedroom and stop near to the wall. As the temperature dropped my heart began to race and I felt panic. The foggy apparition floated about a foot or two above the ground for perhaps 20 or 30 seconds, swirling gently whilst the wind howled outside. As I peered closer, I could make out the figure of a woman, in a long flowing dress with a headscarf and something strapped to her back. At first, I thought it was a deformity, but as it became clearer, I could make out the outline of a basket, just like the one fisherman's wives used to wear when they out at low tide collecting shellfish or sea weed. I watched in astonishment as the figure, now plainly that's of a Fisher Wife, moved silently back towards the door and disappeared.

I sat there for a while, half petrified, half intrigued, listening to the storm outside and wondering if the apparition would make a return appearance. The photographs seemed to glare down at me even more, and I looked closely at them, making out in the half gloom images of hardened, weather beaten Fisher Wives surrounded by baskets of fish and seaweed with unsmiling, grubby children clinging to their skirts. The life of a Victorian Fisherman and his family suddenly seemed less than romantic.

I got very little sleep. The storm finally subsided in the early hours and the next morning I packed and left the cottage with some haste. In the early morning sunshine, the cottage felt completely different. It felt as if a weight had been lifted and the whole atmosphere had changed. As the sunlight streamed through the mullioned windows it passed through a film of dust hanging in the air and for a moment, I thought I saw the faint outline of a figure standing in front of the fire. I hastily left, and closed the door firmly behind me. I didn't look back.

The cottage was an interesting case. I was certain I had seen a ghost in the small hours whilst the storm was raging outside. My initial impression of the cottage was right, there was something unpleasant and unwelcoming in the building and the creepy photographs and blown fuse box only served top convince me of my initial impressions even more. Perhaps this was a recording, or perhaps there really was an intelligent entity at work, making it known that my presence was not wanted!

Haunted Hospitals

What could be scarier than a haunted, Victorian hospital? Disembodied footsteps, a swish of a white coat and a spectral doctor foretelling the imminent death of patients......These stories will chill you to the bone.

During my investigations I have been told a number of stories about hauntings and strange happenings in hospital buildings, particularly the old Victorian Hospitals that were common in Lancashire until a few years ago. Many have now been demolished, such as Blackburn and Clitheroe, to make way for housing and replaced with new, modern hospitals. With so many years of history, it isn't surprising that some old hospitals were home to more than just in-patients!

Marsden Hospital, Burnley

Source – Family Friend

A family friend, Anne, told me stories about Marsden Hospital in Burnley. Opened in around 1899, it was, until 1954, a hospital for infectious diseases and closed in 1992. As a trainee nurse in the 1960's, Anne said that many of the wards felt very spooky and especially at night she often heard noises and footsteps in the corridors. She said expected to see a Doctor or Nurse walking onto the ward but often the footsteps would stop just outside. On one occasion, she heard particularly heavy footsteps approaching her nurses' station but when she went into the corridor to see who was there, she found no-one.

Anne told me she was on duty during the Hapton Pit Disaster of 1962, when injured miners were airlifted to Marsden. 16 Miners lost their lives that day, with two dying from their injuries later. She remembers a long winding staircase down the middle of the building, with wings running off on either side. She said there was always something unsettling about the staircase and that after the disaster, reports of a young man in miner's clothing could be seen leaning over the wrought iron balustrade at the top of the staircase, who disappeared from view when approached.

Blackburn Hospital
Source – Various

The Victorian hospital in Blackburn was built in 1864 on the site of a Workhouse, and expanded greatly in the 1920's. It was renamed Queens Park Hospital and continued to serve Blackburn and the surrounding area until 2006 when a new hospital was opened on the outskirts of the town at a cost of £133 million. The original hospital building, close to Ewood Park, home of Blackburn Rovers Football Club, was renovated and is now a complex of flats and housing. Incidentally, I was born in Queens Park Hospital.

There are many stories associated with the old hospital. Tales of nocturnal footfalls which, when investigated, yield no human presence, and ghostly sightings of long deceased patients echo around the Victorian walls. One particular story, which I was told from a number of contacts via social media, was that of a Doctor who sadly committed suicide in the hospital, only to be regularly seen as a flash of a white coat disappearing around a corner or along a corridor.

On one occasion, a family was gathered around a very poorly relative in a private room when a Doctor in a crisp white coat suddenly entered and asked the family to leave, saying he needed to examine the patient. He left shortly afterwards and sadly the patient passed away not long after the visit. The family asked one of the Nurses who the doctor was, as they wanted to thank him for his kind and considerate bedside manner, but to their surprise the Nurse said no doctor had visited the patient that day, as least, there was no scheduled visit. When they described his appearance the Nurse just stared back blankly. She had no idea who he was!

Other stories relate to this 'Phantom Doctor' and many who worked at the hospital regarded him as a portent of death, as he was often glimpsed in the vicinity shortly before a patient passed away.

Government Buildings (Military Hospital), Norcross, Blackpool

When - 2001

Source – Author

For a while I worked at the Government buildings at Norcross on the outskirts of Blackpool. The site had been a military hospital, built during the Second World War, pre-fabricated and set out in long central corridors with 'spurs' to each side which were used as office space. There were a number of buildings, set out on a large gated complex, and the one I worked in was apparently the most 'interesting' of the buildings. A few colleagues had told me that the building was haunted by patients who had been admitted after the war and died there. I was told of strange happenings and ghostly figures and some of the cleaners refused to go into this particular block alone. Some said you could hear distant wails and screams of patients. The very fabric and layout of the building was depressing and had a coldness to it, even on the warmest of summer days.

Although I had a long 30-mile drive home, I occasionally found myself working late and on my own in the office. I remember one particular early summer evening around 6 o'clock I found myself alone and decided I had done enough for one day and started to tidy my desk. It was still light outside at that time of year.

As I was packing my belongings away, I heard heavy footsteps coming from the corridor and assumed it was either someone working late in one of the other spurs, or a cleaner. As I continued to tidy my desk the footsteps became louder and louder and then suddenly stopped. It was difficult to tell where because the old building would echo, especially footsteps on the tiled floors in the corridors, but it was somewhere near the entrance to my room. Then the footsteps started again, although this time I could hear them getting closer, from within the room, and past right by where I was sat. They seemed to be going towards the far end of the room. Suddenly, and with a deafening crash, the fire door directly to my right, and in the direction of the footsteps, suddenly opened and then slammed shut. For a second I thought I saw a flash of something white.

The door was a purpose-built fire door, it was heavy with a metal bar that needed to be pushed down hard in order to open it. All the doors were checked on a regular basis so it must have been in good working order and I would have noticed if the door wasn't shut properly. I remember thinking at the time that it was strange because it was not windy outside, and there were no open windows in the office to cause a draft. In order to open the door, force would need to be applied to the bar to push it down, thus opening the door, and then considerable force would have been needed to slam the door with such ferocity. I very gingerly walked over to the door and it was indeed now slammed shut, and I tested the bar by pushing down on it and opening the door myself. It seemed to be working as intended and I pulled the door back and locked it. In my opinion, only physical force could have pushed the bar down to open the door, and then apply enough force to slam it shut. The only logical explanation was that some unseen invisible force had caused the door to act in such a way, and that it was paranormal. It was enough to shake me up and I hurriedly gathered my belongings and left.

I mentioned the incident to a few colleagues and that I was convinced the buildings were haunted. One colleague confided in me, whispering that she too had experienced strange things but despite my pressing didn't go into much detail. From my experience, and those of others, I remain convinced that there was a ghostly presence attached to that building and what I witnessed that evening was paranormal activity.

Gisburne Park Hospital, Gisburn.
When – February 2019
Source – Eye Witness accounts and Author

Gisburne Park is situated in the village of Gisburn, which sits on the Lancashire and Yorkshire border on the A59 from Preston to Skipton. It is now a private hospital, although it also takes non private patients from around the area for routine operations and day cases. Situated in 1000 acres of Lancashire countryside, it is also a holiday park and equestrian centre.

Gisburne Park was built in the 18th century and is a Grade I listed building. The land was first acquired by the Lister family in the 16th century, and it was Thomas Lister, 1st Baron Ribblesdale, who built the Hall between 1727 and 1736. Lister was the

Member of Parliament for Clitheroe from 1713 until his death in 1745, when the Hall was passed to his son, Thomas (1723 – 1761) who was also the Member of Parliament for Clitheroe following his father's death. He was responsible for planting over a million oak trees throughout the Ribble Valley. The hall then passed down through a succession of Thomas Lister's until the passing of Thomas Lister, 4th Baron of Ribblesdale in 1925. Part of the estate was then sold to cover death duties as Thomas's two sons had both been killed in action – one in the Boer War and the other in the 1st World War. Part of the estate was bought by the Hindley Family, who founded the shop chain British Home Stores. In 1995 the Hall and surrounding grounds were sold to become the BMI Gisburne Park Hospital.

In February of 2019, as I was writing this book, I was admitted to Gisburne Park Hospital for a routine operation to remove a small lump from my right hand. Whilst I was recovering from the effects of a General Anaesthetic, I started chatting to a few of the nursing staff and mentioned I was writing this book. To my surprise, I was told that Gisburne Park had its own ghost, believed to that of the first Thomas Lister and that he had been seen many times, by members of staff and patients. He had been seen floating down the corridor which connected the in-patient ward with the main entrance hall and reception. Numerous paintings of him hang in the building and his spirit is easily recognisable from these likenesses, he is even dressed in period clothes. One of the nurses also told me that 'Orbs' are often seen in this corridor, which is the oldest part of the building.

Although I was sent home on the day of my operation, complications meant that I had to return the following day for assessment. I was admitted back to the same room, and as I was lying on the day listening to the radio, I noticed a 'sparkle' of light down to my left, below the line of the bed near to the floor. The best way of describing it was like a firework sparkler, and although it only lasted for a few seconds it was long enough for me to look directly at it before it disappeared as quickly as it has appeared.

The room I was staying in turned out to be on the corridor where orbs had been seen. I have thought about this incident and what may have caused it. I wear glasses, so it may have been a lens flare from the window to my right (although it was an overcast day and overlooked some gardens, so it couldn't have been car headlights), and the lights in the room were subdued and consistent, with no flickering or other anomalies. In all my years of wearing spectacles, I have never had a similar lens flare or visual anomaly like it.

Did I really see an orb, or something similar, or was it just a trick of the light? I would like to think it was Thomas Lister paying me a visit.

The Strange Story of Huntroyd Hall, Simonstone

In 1594 there was a demonic possession of eight people, and a Witch was employed to rid them of their evil spirits!

Huntroyd Hall circ 1880. : © W Farrer and J Brownbill eds. – The Victoria History of the County of Lancaster Vol 6, Public Domain.

The village of Simonstone lies 4 miles west of Burnley and to the south of Pendle Hill. Today, it is bustling with businesses and residents, but in the 16th century it was small farming community centred on Huntroyd Hall.

In 1594 there took place a most perplexing episode that had roots in witchcraft and local folklore. Taking place a full 18 years before the infamous trial of the Lancashire Witches, Nicholas Starkie and his wife lived in the large house with their two children, John and Anne. No fewer than 7 people were to become victim of demonic possession and the children were the first to be afflicted by evil spirits. Starkie summoned an exorcist by the name of Edmund Hartlay, who rapidly dealt with the spirits by the use of magical spells. However, once the children were 'cured' he refused to leave convincing Starkie that only his continued presence in the house would prevent a recurrence of the trouble. He even went so far as to demand forty shillings a year, on top of his free accommodation.

Why Starkie employed Hartlay is a mystery. Hartlay was known as the 'Tyldsley Witch', and had resided at Cleworth Hall, seat of Lady Starkie's family, for many years. He was described as a 'fearsome and cunning man'.

Three years later, Nicholas Starkie was growing increasingly tired of his house-guest and told Hartlay he must leave. Legend goes that there was a heated argument, during which it became apparent that the two children were once again possessed. To make it worse, two of the servants started acting possessed as did Starkie's three female wards and an innocent visitor to the house! All eight began shouting and shrieking, running around babbling and foaming at the mouth. In the confusion and panic, Starkie blamed Hartlay claiming that he had breathed the Devil into whoever he had kissed in greeting. The 'possessions' lasted for days. The afflicted women and children suffered terrifying delusions such as imagining beasts were inside their own bodies, seeing huge angry dogs and hearing gravelly, demonic voices. They ran about madly and one even tried to hurl herself from a window. They spoke in strange tongues at great speed, howling and shaking with fear.

Dr John Dee was Queen Elizabeth I's own astrologer and alchemist and was called to assist in exorcising the afflicted. Unfortunately for Starkie he refused to be involved saying that it was 'conjuring' on the part of Hartlay. He suggested that religious men should be summoned to deal with the exorcisms instead.

The two ministers who attended were George More and John Darrell and it is the latter who wrote a detailed account of what happened next. More and Darrell gathered all the demoniacs together (a name they invented to describe the poor people involved) and laid them on couches. They brought thirty religious people to pray with them for an entire day, hoping to drive out the devils. By the next day, amazingly all eight were seemingly demon free, although some of them were reported to bleed from the mouth and nose as the deliverance occurred.

As Edmund Hartlay was clearly responsible for the so-called 'demonic possessions', he was tried for witchcraft at Lancaster Castle. At first, the judge could find no basis on which to convict him, despite the trouble he had caused. Starkie came forward and swore to the judge that he had seen Hartlay draw a magic circle into which he had invited Starkie to step. This kind of witchcraft was a felony so, as much as Hartlay denied doing anything of the kind, he was sentenced to death! Quite clearly, the testament of one very aggrieved Gentleman of means was enough to sentence another to death.

It is worth noting the religious knife edge that many well-to-do families were perched on during the Tudor times. First the Protestants were persecuted, then the Catholics.

Although Elizabeth I tried to shy away from mass religious murder as her Father and Sister had been so keen on, there was still hatred and mistrust of those not of the same faith as the Protestant Queen. Darrell wrote his accounts and accused the family of Lady Starkie, who had been married before to Thomas Barton of Smithells Hall. They were accused of bringing about the whole affair by their prayers. They were Catholics and were said to have prayed for the death of all Lady Starkie's male children from both her marriages, so that their lands and titles would not be inherited by them. Whatever the reason, Starkie's two children John and Anne suffered no lasting damage from their demonic experience. Anne grew up and married happily, and John became Sheriff of Lancashire.

As for Edmund Hartlay, he was hanged in March 1697. He was hanged twice, just to make sure.

Boggarts and more Boggarts!

Nasty, malicious spirits hell bent of causing misery and destruction. Nasty little spirits lurking at every gate post and in every pond. Boggarts under bridges, in canals and the headless dog Boggart of Preston!

Evil Boggart © Craig Bryant

As a child I was fascinated by the stories of mischievous spirits lurking around every tree or in every slimy green pond. In Lancashire. These horrible and frightening creatures were called 'Boggarts'.

A Boggart is a malevolent or mischievous spirit. Taken from the old English 'Bar Gheist' or 'Gate Ghost', Lancashire has many sites attributed to these mean and nasty spirits. In modern times, household Boggarts have been renamed as Poltergeists but their outdoor dwelling cousins still instil fear and furtive glances from the old folk of Lancashire as they hurry down dark country lanes on windswept nights.

In olden days, the best way to placate a Boggart was to give it a saucer of milk or banish it underground and plant a Holly bush on top of it. On a lane near Longridge is a stone slab, known as the 'Written Stone' dated 1655, with a Holly planted next to it. The inscription reads 'RAVFFE RADCLIFF LAID THIS STONE TO LYE FOREVER A.D 1655'. Local legend tells of how a malevolent Boggart terrorised people by physically attacking them, and was deemed responsible for the death of a family member of Radcliffe's from nearby Radcliffe Farm. Radcliffe dealt with the creature by laying it under the stone. The legend goes on that the next owner of this farm decided he wanted possession of the Written Stone and it is said that it took six horses and many men to remove the stone and deliver to the farm, where it was placed in the dairy. Over time things started happening, accidents happened to people who came into contact with the stone and objects placed on the stone would be pushed off and damaged. The farmer started to believe the stories of a Boggart attached to the stone slab and came to the conclusion that it was cursed and must be returned. When he finally decided to return it to its original place, it only took one horse and a couple of men to return it whereas before it had taken a tremendous effort to move it!

Boggart Hole Clough in Radcliffe, near Manchester, is well known locally as a beauty spot to avoid after dark. Plagued by a spirit with a high shrill voice, a local farmer and his family was tormented to such a degree that they hurriedly loaded up a cart and were about to 'do a flit' (move house) when a voice cried out that it was coming with them! Knowing full well that the spirit would follow them, they decided to stay put.

Priestly Clough in Accrington was also known locally as Boggart Clough (a 'clough' is a local term for a small, often wooded valley). A local saying was "*Ee's set off a t'Boggart!*" meaning a quick footed or spring heeled individual. This naughty spirit was indeed 'spring heeled', and children playing in the clough would occasionally catch site of it peering around trees waiting to pounce on any child that ventured too close. The spirit would grab its victims and push them into the stream that flowed through the clough. The mischievous Imp was also supposed to cause an ancient old oak tree to uproot and stomp around the woodland on stormy nights! Children knew of this this as the legend of 'The Walking Tree'.

There is also a legend which tells of a river Boggart living under Grindleton Bridge on the River Ribble, near Chatburn. In times gone by, before the invention of motor cars, children were warned not to play on the river banks near the bridge just in case the Boggart grabbed them by the ankles and dragged them to a watery grave. Similar stories are told of Brungerley Bridge, further down the river, where the ghost of a young girl is often seen gliding along the river bank as well as a Boggart that terrorised travellers at Roach Bridge near Salmesbury.

At the back of Towneley Hall is the old road which stretched between Bacup and Todmorden and is today part of the network of visitor pathways. Part of the road is named Boggart Bridge which crosses a small stream.

A particularly objectionable and troublesome Boggart once lived here who demanded gifts from the travellers before they were allowed to cross. If they refused, it would grab them by the ankles and drown them in the brook, disposing of their bodies by eating them.

After years of torment, the locals hatched a plan. They offered a compromise whereby the Boggart could keep the soul of the first living thing that crossed the bridge the following day. In agreeing to this it would also agree to 'never again appear as long as there was greenery around'. The Boggart greedily agreed.

The trap was set. Next day the local folk sent over an old hen which the Boggart pounced on and killed. Realising it had been fooled, but unable to break its promise; it disappeared in a puff of smoke leaving behind the smell of brimstone and sulphur.

Quickly, the locals planted Holly bushes around the bridge and the Boggart has been silent ever since.

The Black Dog of Preston, a huge headless Boggart, roamed Preston's streets and lanes for centuries. It's disembodied howling could be heard all around the town and was often accompanied by the rattling of chains. It was said it was the harbinger of death and anyone unlucky enough to hear it would suffer a horrible fate. This spectral hound is also associated with Gallows Hill in Preston, where 16 Jacobite rebels were hung in chains after the Battle of Preston in 1715. It's form had been seen near this place of death, swaying from side to side and pawing the air, letting out a blood curdling howl in the process. Interestingly, the English Martyr's Church now stands on the summit of Gallows Hill. Nearby Derwentwater Place and Lovat Road refer to Jacobites captured and executed during the rebellion. During the building of North Road which cuts through the hill, workmen found two headless bodies. The area is also known as 'Provincial Tyburn'.

The Leeds to Liverpool canal winds its way through the Lancashire countryside connecting the port of Liverpool in the west, to the urban conurbations of Manchester and Leeds in the east. Once a thriving thoroughfare of trade, the working canal boats have long gone to be replaced by pleasure craft and residential narrow boats. My maternal great grandfather worked the canal barges at the turn of the 20th century, and my grandfather Bill told me that as a child he was deterred from playing near to the canal with warnings a Boggart called 'Ginny Greenteeth' who lurked under the swing bridge at Church. Shaped like a horseshow, the canal basin at Church was a loading and unloading point for coal and finished cotton for the local weaving mills. Deeper than the canal at either side, it was said that if you fell in the weeds along the bottom would reach up and entangle your legs, pulling you down and drowning you in a few minutes. Worse still, Ginny Greenteeth would wait under the swing bridge and pull children down to a watery grave. My grandfather said as children they were genuinely frightened of the tale. No local child went swimming in the canal, or skated on it during the coldest winters. If you did, Greenteeth would 'ave you! As a somewhat rebellious child, I often played near the canal and on the swing bridge, much to the annoyance of my grandparents, peering over the wooden railing to see if I could catch a glimpse of the evil Boggart, but I never did!

Ley Lines

Can supernatural lines of energy across the landscape intersect and cause surges of paranormal energy that throw people out of time? Could they be UFO highways, or centres of paranormal activity?

Put simply, Ley Lines are ancient lines of power or paranormal energy that link places or objects, always in a straight line. It is likely that these lines are natural phenomena; perhaps minerals in the earth somehow concentrate energy. Indeed, the area around The Rossendale Valley in the south of Lancashire is rich in mineral deposits, and also rich in UFO sightings. The valley itself lies on a line which runs North West to South East from Castlerigg Stone Circle in Cumbria, through Pendle Hill and down to Manchester.

There is also a theory that where these Ley Lines cross, particularly strong localised phenomena can occur, in particular time slips, portals to other dimensions, UFO sightings and other such weird occurrences. Lancashire is replete with ley lines, with a number of significant crossing points where two lines meet.

Some people believe that ley lines are ancient pagan ceremonial 'high ways', established routes that people followed when large groups of people gathered for religious purposes, such as the summer and winter solstices. Atop Pendle Hill is an ancient Bronze Age burial site, and a ley line is reputed to bisect the Hill into two, right through this ancient site. One theory is that these straight lines marked a path to important resources such as ore, flint or salt.

Ley lines have long been associated with paranormal and UFO activity. The points where they cross are particularly powerful and this alignment of energy is supposed to bring on all sorts of strange phenomena including UFO 'highways' and time slips.

<u>The Bold Street Time Slips</u>

Some of the most famous, and intriguing, instances of time slips have happened in Liverpool on Bold Street in the city centre. The most famous story involved an ex police officer named Frank. One afternoon they were out shopping in Liverpool and his wife decided that she wanted to go and buy a book at Waterstones, the large book store on Bold Street, and they started to walk towards the area where the shop was.

As they approached Bold Street, Frank decided he wanted to go to another shop first, but bumped into a friend and stopped to chat in the street. His wife went ahead without him.

A few moments later, Frank said goodbye, went to his shop and came out again to go to Waterstones meet his wife. After reaching Bold Street, he headed on towards the bookstore. As he approached Waterstones he looked up and was surprised to see the name 'Cripps' above the door. As he was about to cross the street a van drove past him with the name Cardin's on the side. The van drive honked his old-fashioned horn to warn him he was there and drove past.

Looking around, Frank suddenly realised that things were not quite how they should be. He noticed the cars driving past were all old-fashioned vehicles land looked like they belonged in the 1950's or 1960's. As he watched the cars he suddenly noticed that the people were all dressed strangely too - the men were all wearing hats and old fashioned Mackintosh jackets, and the women were dressed in head scarves, full skirts and had old fashioned hair styles, exactly like the ones popular just after the war.

Frank was beginning to feel things were most definitely not right, but he carried on crossing the road and headed towards where Waterstones should have been.

As he got closer, he noticed that instead of books, the windows were full of handbags, shoes and umbrellas. Suddenly he saw a young woman at his side looking up at the shop sign with a look of confusion on her face.

Frank noticed that this young woman was wearing modern clothes and as she looked at him, she smiled. Frank went into the shop, closely followed by the young women. When they entered, he was surprised, and relieved, to see that they were stood in Waterstones, surrounded by piles of books. The young women looked quizzically at Frank and smiled, shook her head and said, 'that was strange, I thought it was a new clothes shop!'. She turned and walked out of the shop, looking extremely puzzled.

What is peculiar about this story is that according to Frank's account of the incident, it would seem that he was not the only one momentarily transported back in time and that the young woman who accompanied him into the shop was also 'out of time' and equally as confused as he was. Interestingly, Cripps was indeed a store that occupied the sight of Waterstones many years earlier, and Cardin's was a firm that owned a fleet of vans in Liverpool about the same time.

There are other instances of time shifts associated with ley lines. There is a crossing of lines at Starr Gate, in between Lytham St Annes and Blackpool. Here, all manner of strange phenomena has been reported including phantom trams and people dressed in Victorian clothing as well as a number of UFO sightings. Although there is a British Aerospace aircraft testing facility close by at Wharton, they have denied any activity that coincides with unexplained sightings.

The Winter Hill UFO Incident

Two ley lines also allegedly cross Winter Hill on the West Pennine Moors near Bolton. This is an area of ancient mystery and legends and a hotbed of UFO activity. On Saturday 13th November 1999 a local UFO Investigator, Steve Mera, received a telephone call from a very distressed cattle hand called Stuart Murphy who told him that there was a strange light in the sky and he was very frightened. Mr Murphy went on to say that he had been working on the farm as a cattle hand for 15 years, and on this particular afternoon he was going about his business when suddenly he heard a loud droning sound coming from above. As he looked up, he noticed a bright light in the sky over a field full of his cattle. He went on to explain that the object just hung in the sky whilst the cattle ran around in panic. After a short while the object moved away and, fearing for the safety of his livestock, Mr Murphy ran up to the field. As he entered through the gate he looked up and saw to his horror that the object was moving back toward him. Panicking, he turned and ran as fast as he could back towards his farmhouse with the object now directly above him and, according to Mr Murphy, 'only a few feet above him'. As he entered the farm house he looked back and saw the object hovering directly over the field again. He immediately rang Greater Manchester Police who initially did not take him seriously. Mr Murphy had quite a strong Irish accent and in his agitated state was difficult to understand according to Mr Mera. The police knew of the investigators local organisation and gave Mr Murphy his telephone number, hence the call to him. It was only the following day that he properly spoke to Mr Murphy about what had happened.

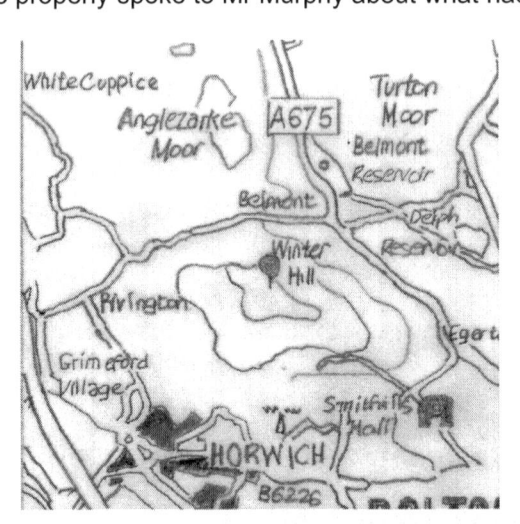

Location of Winter Hill © Craig Bryant

According to Mr Murphy, a short while after the incident he was visited by three suited gentleman who claimed to be from the Department for Agriculture, Fisheries and Food. He said they looked like the 'Men in Black'. They were extremely interested in Mr Murphy's story and warned him not to divulge it to anyone else. He told Mr Mera that this left him very shook up and that he felt they were threatening him. They said harm would come to him and his family if he spoke to anyone about the incident and that if he didn't cooperate the farm would be closed down. As it was not Mr Murphy's farm, and the owner was none too pleased for these gentlemen to show up unannounced investigating such wild stories, Mr Murphy was frightened. Interestingly, when he met the investigator, he explained that he knew talking to him could be risky, but that he needed to tell someone the story. He also had a red, itchy mark on his cheek that had appeared shortly afterwards and he could not explain how he got it. Not long after the incident, he and his family moved back to Ireland. The investigator continued to make enquiries into the incident but hit numerous dead ends. He spoke to the local police officers with little success and held a number of stakeouts on the farm itself but did not see any further incidents. During this time, Mr Mera claims that whilst he was locating the farm for the first time, he was followed by a jeep which pulled into a small car park behind him. The driver, a man in his mid 30's and dressed in jeans, a jumper and cap, got out and started questioning him about what he was doing, and why he was so interested in that particular farm. Mr Mera told him he was looking for a friend's farm and with that the man in the jeep got back in his vehicle and sped off.

After much investigation Mr Mera located the farm near to the village of Tockholes on the Chorley side of the hill, known locally as 'Andrews Farm'. He noticed a field full of cattle, and a dark burnt patch in centre which he thought was unusual. When he approached the farm, he met the owner who categorically denied anything had happened, that he did not know Stuart Murphy and that he had been told not to discuss the matter further. During the conversation, Mr Mera states that a number of vehicles arrived at the farm, including the same jeep that he had encountered earlier, with the same driver. At this point he left and decided to shelve his investigation pending further developments. The final part of his report states that although there have been other UFO sightings over the years in the Winter Hill area, no further evidence regarding Mr Murphy's encounter has come to light.

This incident is fascinating. There have been a number of strange sightings over Winter Hill but this is one of the more perplexing. What exactly did Mr Murphy see? Was it a UFO or just a commercial aircraft, such as helicopter? If so, why was it taking such an interest in this field, and why did the 'Men in Black' arrive shortly afterward reputedly from a Government Ministry? Why did they threaten Mr Murphy? Who was the man in the jeep and why was he so keen to track Mr Mera? Finally, what caused the farm owner to flatly deny the incident had happened or that he did not know a cattle hand who had worked for him for 15 years?

Short Stories

A collection of spine-chilling mysteries, from haunted stairways, to spectral figures in the road. Ghostly Pike in a long, deserted lodge, poltergeists and a repeating ghost nicknamed Henrietta!

The Man in the Flat Cap

Source – Work Colleague

When – 1990's

A work colleague told me a fascinating story that had happened to her and her husband a number of years ago. She said she couldn't remember the exact date, but it was sometime in the early 1990's.

She recounted that she and her husband were driving home in the early hours of New Years Day along Marsh Road from Freckleton to Preston. Freckleton lies on the north bank of the Ribble estuary, along a series of tidal inlets. A public House, the Ship Inn, lies on one of these inlets and many legends tell of smugglers sailing silently up the creeks on moonless nights to unload their illegal contraband at the Pub.

My colleague told that she was driving, and approaching the traffic lights with the main A583 road when she suddenly saw a man in a flat cap appeared in front of her car. Unable to stop, she was convinced had hit him and that he had gone over the bonnet of the car. However, she remembered there was no bump or sound of any sort and when she stopped the car and looked in her rear-view mirror, half expecting to see a prostate body in the road, there was nothing there. She said she asked her husband if he too saw the man and he confirmed he had. She said it felt so real, and was convinced that this man had gone over the bonnet of the car but on inspection there was absolutely no one there

"Henrietta"

Source – Family Member

Close to the Holden Arms, on the Grane Road from Haslingden to Blackburn, is an old farm house situated next to a Graveyard. The church has been converted into an Antiques shop but it is unknown whether any of the bodies were reinterred or moved. I have been told of a farm house close by, with its own resident female spirit, named 'Henrietta'. The house was owned by Mr Billy Grimshaw, and it was he who nicknamed her Henrietta. She was very active and manifested herself on a regular basis in one of the bedrooms. My source tells me she wasn't malevolent, and caused no injury or harm. Henrietta has been seen many times standing at the bottom of the bed and Billy tells her off, shouting at her to leave him alone, which invariably she does!

Henrietta became so famous locally that the BBC actually sent a film crew but sadly she decided not to perform for the cameras. No sooner had they left though, than she appeared yet again!

The Accrington Poltergeist
Source – Various
When – 1970's

A council house on Queensway in Church, near Accrington, is reportedly the scene of some terrifying poltergeist activity. The house is situated near to St Christopher's School, across from Dill Hall Cemetery. When I was a teenager, I attended the school and later my family moved to the area and I remember being told about a haunted house close by that families never seemed to live in for long. These stories went as far back as the 1970's, although the earliest written record I can find is in the Accrington Observer newspaper from 2003. By all accounts the Council becoming so fed up with tenants leaving that they hired a local priest to exorcise the house, but to no avail and several audio recordings were made of paranormal activity during the attempt.

In early 1990's, according to the Accrington Observer, a mother of four was so terrified of living in the house that she abandoned it with her children and begged the Council to re-home her. For a second time, an exorcist was called in, but again to no avail – the Poltergeist refused to co-operate. Reports state that a guitar started playing itself, family members were grabbed by freezing cold unseen hands and a bath spontaneously filled itself with water (no problems with the taps or plumbing could be found). A former resident told the newspaper that as they were about to leave for the last time, the front door was closed so tightly that they couldn't open it, having to hurriedly leave by the back door. Obviously, something didn't want them to vacate the house!

Whilst I was researching this particular subject, I was contacted by a lady through social media whose Grandmother had lived near by and said that the house had a 'bad ghost'. She remembered being told about the 'haunted house' as a child and said that if an adult tried to enter the bedroom at the front of the house they would be physically flung out. Whatever the entity was it would only allow children in the room……

The Haunted Stairway
Location – A House in Bury, Greater Manchester
When – 1990's
Source – Owner of the house and Author's experience

Although Bury is now a town in Greater Manchester, it was once part of Lancashire before the boundary changes so I make no apology for including this particular story in a book about Lancashire ghosts!

My girlfriend at the time lived with her mother, younger sister and step father in a three-story house in Bury. Although I am unsure of the age of the building, it was probably early to mid Victorian era. I was large house, built over three storeys and on the end of a terrace of similar houses. When built, it would probably have been a fairly well-off families' residence, no doubt involved in the cotton industry which was important to so many Lancashire town during the 19th century.

There was always a strange feeling in the house. It had an unpleasant atmosphere, and not just because my girlfriend's step dad obviously didn't like me much! The house seemed to have a heavy atmosphere to it, and I distinctly remember how oppressive the front of the house felt, even with the light streaming in through the old Victorian bay window. There always seemed to be dust hanging in the air, despite the fact that the house was kept clean and dust free.

The stairway from the ground to the first floor was particularly unpleasant. It was narrow, steep and dark and always felt colder than any other part of the house. My girlfriend's mother told me that on several occasions, she had been walking down the stairs and felt someone was following her. She said that it happened mostly first thing in the morning when she was walking down the stairs in her dressing gown, and would often feel like she was being shoved down the stairs, not in a way to make her fall forwards, but to 'hurry' her along. Apparently, no other member of the family or guests ever had a similar experience.

The Brown Cow Public House

Location – Chatburn

Source –Previous Landlady

When – Mid 2000's

The village of Chatburn is situated close to the Market town of Clitheroe in The Ribble Valley in East Lancashire. It is overlooked by Pendle Hill on one side, and the Bowland Fells on the other.

The Brown Cow, Chatburn © Craig Bryant.

Of the two pubs in the village, the Brown Cow is the larger, although the Black Bull is a lovely cosy little pub with snugs and open fires, and a decent selection of beers. Over the past 10 years or so The Brown Cow has had a number of tenant landlords, until its renovation a couple of years ago. It is now a 'gastropub' that sells really good food and beers, with open fires and a nice homely feel.

The pub itself dates back to the 1850's and was coaching house situated on a toll road which, before the main A59 bypass was built, was part of a road that linked Bury and Skipton in order to transport lime from the numerous lime kilns that were around Skipton in the 19th century. As an aside, the road was one of many built by 'Blind' Jack Metcalfe from Knaresborough in Yorkshire. The old Tollhouse is still in the village, situated on the corner of Downham Road and is now Hudson's famous Ice Cream shop.

The Brown Cow still has the large dining room which Sarah and I hired for our wedding reception in 2006, although following the renovations the layout has changed. As we were planning our wedding, I asked the landlady if the pub had any paranormal activity, and was not surprised to hear that it did! Before the current renovations, the bar was situated to the left of the entrance, with a corridor behind leading to the dining room. This corridor had now become integrated into the main entrance to the pub and the bar turned 90 degrees to be face on when entering through the main doors. However, the story I was told was that the ghost of a small boy had been seem by previous tenants of the pub running up and down the corridor, and that he was dressed very much in the fashion of a stable boy from late Victorian times. The ghost didn't seem to respond to anyone, and from his description he seems to be a 'replay' type of spirit. Whether he has been seen after the renovations is a question I must ask next time I pop in for a pint or a meal!

Government Buildings

Location – Preston

Source – Security Guards

When – Present day

Situated on a busy junction in the centre of Preston, St Mary's House is now owned by HM Revenue and Customs. It was previously built and owned by North West Water, the predecessor of United Utilities. The building is situated next to the now redundant St Mary's Anglican Church (the church was closed in 2006), and is now a conservation centre for the Museum of Lancashire. The church itself was constructed between 1836 and 1838 by John Latham.

Part of the graveyard backs on the outer perimeter of St Mary's House and a number of bodies were moved and reinterred following the closure of the church. When HMRC took lease of the building in the early 2000's renovation work was carried out to bring the offices up to modern standard. Security guards are employed on a 24-hour basis and one now retired guard told me that there were some 'spooky goings-on' in the building, especially at night but occasionally during the day. These manifested themselves as heavy footsteps and banging noises, sometimes from the ground floor but often from the first, directly above where the guards were situated. Occasionally footsteps could be heard stomping through the corridors during the daytime; even though no employees were in the vicinity and one of the guards told me he felt very uneasy checking the floors late at night to make sure nobody was working later than they should. One of the guards I spoke to dismissed the stories as 'rubbish' and said that it was just the building 'settling' every night, and that the bangs were just the heating system cooling down after being turned off for the night. The retired guard I spoke to maintained, however, that there was something definitely ghostly going on in the building and that he was convinced it was somehow connected to St Mary's church next door

Jacobs Lodge and the Ghostly Pike
Location – Green Howarth, Accrington
Source – Local legend

Jacobs Lodge is a small area of outstanding natural beauty, high up on the moors near to Green Howarth in Accrington. Standing some 900 feet above sea level it has spectacular views westward towards the Fylde Coast, especially on a clear day.

A 'Lodge', in local dialect, is a small body of water. Jacob's Lodge is indeed small in diameter, but legend has it that the lodge is very deep. As a child and teenager, I used to fish the lodge with friends, as it was only a short walk from my house up the lane and over the fields. Legend also told of a monstrous phantom Pike which inhabited the Lodge and would drag unsuspecting waterfowl and occasionally small dogs down to its murky depths. Many a furtive evening was spent in late summer, sat silently on the banks of the lodge watching a fishing float whilst hoping to catch a glimpse of the Phantom Pike. Sadly, neither I nor any of my friends ever did.

I remember one evening a man was walking his small Yorkshire Terrier along the bank by a lead, refusing to let it off despite its protestations. He told us his previous dog had jumped in the Lodge for a swim, only to suddenly violently splash around and disappear under the surface without a trace. Maybe it was just a very large Pike, after all, they can grow big in the right conditions, but in such a small body of water with limited food supply? No, I like to think that the Ghostly Pike was responsible and it still cruises just below the surface on moonlit nights, waiting for its next meal!

The Piano

When – Present Day

Source – Author

My wife, Sarah, is very musical. She comes from a family of musicians – her parents and uncle played in a professional band in the 1980's and Sam, her maternal grandfather was a choirmaster and organist in Liverpool. Sarah herself plays the Cello and the piano, and has rather a good singing voice (she takes after her mother in that respect).

A few years ago, Sarah decided to buy a second hand piano. The upright, which she bought from a shop in Clitheroe specialising in second hand piano's, was so heavy that it took six full grown men to manoeuvre it through the front door and in to the dining room. Although it is undoubtedly a beautiful piece of furniture, for some reason I never felt comfortable near it, despite enjoying looking at it. It was only a couple of years later when we employed a piano tuner that we discovered its provenance.

Under the lid is a plaque which gives the date of manufacture as 1911 by Blüthner, of Leipzig. Furthermore, it had a serial number.

I contacted the UK office of Blüthner who kindly gave me some additional information, in that the Piano was made of Rosewood and had been sold to a Manchester dealer 'Hime and Addisons' in 1911. The retailer is no more, but had been situated on Deansgate in Manchester City Centre. They further told me that they had a record of the piano being bought and serviced by them in a house in Rossendale, Lancashire in 1977 but that was the last record they held. This tied in with the retailer Sarah purchased the piano from, as they said they had acquired it from a house in Rossendale, and that it had been in that family for years.

Sarah does not believe me when I say the piano has brought her bad luck. She has had a terrible run of fortune in her professional life as a teacher, and has a number of enforced job changes since she bought it. I believe there is *something* attached to the piano, although nothing paranormal has happened that I can directly attribute to it.

James also plays the piano. A few weeks ago (as I write this chapter) he was in the dining room one evening, practising playing the piano, only to later tell us that he saw a 'mist' (as he described it) in the room as he entered. We quizzed him on it but he could not really say any more. It is noticeable that the dining room, being north west facing, is always extremely cold even in the hottest of summers and was, prior to our buying the house and renovating it, a downstairs bedroom. Perhaps something lingers in the room, or perhaps my assertions are right and something has, indeed, attached itself to the piano.

Famously Haunted Lancashire

Ghostly stories of Old Lancashire. Spectral hounds, phantom hitchhikers, white ladies and fairies. Lancashire has it all!

The County of Lancashire covers an area of roughly 1,189 square miles (3,080 square kilometres) and is situated in the north west of England. It borders Cumbria to the north, Greater Manchester and Merseyside to the south, and North and West Yorkshire to the east; with a coastline on the Irish Sea to the west. Its terrain varies greatly, from lowland farm land in the west and south, to moorland to the north and east. On its eastern boarders rise The Pennine Hills, and to the north the Yorkshire Dales and the Limestone hills of Pen-Y-Ghent, Whernside and Ingleborough.

Its most famous peak is Pendle Hill, but to the north, through the Bowland Fells to the border with Cumbria, are some more spectacular, if less fabled, hills. Wards Stone rises to 563 metres (1,841 feet), a full 4 metres higher than its more southerly cousin and is a magnet for walkers and fell runners alike. This is the highest point in the Forest of Bowland.

The history of Lancashire can be traced back to the 12th Century, although there were occupied Roman outposts such as Ribchester and Manchester hundreds of years before that. Up to the Industrial Revolution it was thought of as a fairly lawless place, making a living from the land was hard and it was a sparsely populated area. It was not until the Industrial Revolution that Lancashire began to grow in importance, with towns such as Accrington, Blackburn, Burnley and Oldham becoming centres of Industrial entrepreneurism thanks to the cotton industry. Manchester became fabulously wealthy on the back of cotton, earning the nickname 'Cottonopolis' and the Port of Liverpool became one of the busiest in the world. First canals, then steam railways sprung up throughout the county as the Industrial Revolution gained pace. The Leeds to Liverpool Canal is still navigable to narrow boats today, although no small thanks to the programme of dredging and restoration that took place in the 1980's and 1990's after the system had fallen into disrepair.

To the west lies the Fylde Coast, north of the Ribble Estuary, with its most famous town of Blackpool which grew up as a favourite holiday destination for the thousands of Victorian Mill workers on their annual 'Wakes Weeks'. These were traditional holiday weeks when entire towns would shut down, including factories, mills and shops. Of course, each town would have its own particular week when thousands of its workers would leave the dark, smoky mills behind for a week of fun by the seaside. Other towns, such as Morecambe, situated on its famous bay and River Kent Estuary grew to accommodate this growing bands of holiday seekers, as well as slightly more up market and genteel resorts such as Southport, just to the north of Liverpool.

Lancashire is famous for many things. Historically, Dunsop Bridge lay at the dead centre of Britain. More recently, according to the Ordnance Survey Map, this is actually in a field near Calderstones, Whalley. Personally, I think the former is slightly more romantic! Another little-known fact is that JRR Tolkein based his Lord of the Rings books, in particular his vision of 'Middle Earth', on the Ribble Valley and surrounding area after spending time at Stoneyhurst College, a private Jesuit school located on the Stoneyhurst Estate near Clitheroe.

Lancashire is steeped in history and legend. You can find dozens of Stately Halls and Haunted Houses, each boastings its own ghost or ghosts. Salmesbury Hall, now situated on the A59 Blackburn and Preston road, boasts perhaps the most famous – Dorothy DeSouthworth, better known as the White Lady. She has been seen crossing the road as a filmy shape by numerous motorists, several of which have reported hitting a young girl in their car as she suddenly appeared out of nowhere.

Turton Tower near Bolton is residence to two 'Screaming Skulls' which do not like to be moved. They were fished out from nearby Bradshaw Brook in 1750 and placed on the mantelpiece at nearby Timberbottom Farm. Whenever they were moved there would be violent poltergeist activity and it was only when the farm as demolished were they moved to Bradshaw Hall, and then to Turton when that was also demolished. One of the skulls is nearly whole and appears to have been slashed by a sharp instrument. The other is a fragment. Both sit happily on the Bradshaw family Bible, rescued before demolition. It is safe to say no one dares to move them!

Towneley Hall in Burnley has its own resident ghostly Lord of The Manor, Sir John Towneley who died in 1541. This land grabbing spirit is often seen wandering the corridors of the Hall, and is occasionally seen in the grounds. When alive he illegally seized large tracks of land from the local commoners and farmers, depriving them of grazing and turning it into his own private hunting estate.

Chingle Hall, in Chipping near Preston, was once called England's most haunted house. It is now a private residence, and by all accounts the current owner is none too happy for visitors to arrive unannounced hoping to catch a glimpse of the fabled Black Monk. Over the years, this phantom has made many a guest flee in terror, including an Italian Prisoner of War during World War Two who was billeted at Chingle. Following his first night at the Hall he refused to stay in his assigned bedroom again, exclaiming, "Spirit in room! I no stay!"

There are haunted pubs galore. The Sun Inn, also at Chipping, is haunted by Lizzie Dean who hanged herself after being jilted on her wedding day. Landlord William Southworth, who was murdered in 1820 at the Buck Inn at Waddington, is still reputedly seen to this day. The Parkers Arms at Newton- in- Bowland has not one, but two resident ghosts – one of a little old lady seen around the bar and the other of a man without legs outside in the grounds! It brings a whole new meaning to the phrase 'being legless' I suppose!

The DeLacy Arms in Whalley has its very own spectral White Monk, and The Swan and Royal in Clitheroe is supposed to be haunted by the sad ghost of 17-year-old local girl Anne Druce, who fell pregnant to a soldier billeted there during the Cotton Riots of 1878. They had arranged to marry, but he was sent to Africa and was killed. Wracked with grief, Anne hanged herself in the very bedroom they had shared together. There is also a small cot which reputedly rocks by itself in one of the guest rooms.

The Swan and Royal is also famous for Sir Frank Whittle of jet engine fame who stayed there whilst he was working in secret at a factory in Clitheroe set up by the Lucas company. Sir Winston Churchill also stayed in the hotel whilst visiting Whittle's factory. Other famous guests have included Ian Anderson of Jethro Tull fame, and Miss Whiplash the famous 'Dominatrix to the Stars' who stood for MP in the Ribble Valley constituency in the 1991 General Election.

Sawley Abbey © Craig Bryant

Sawley Abbey, situated close to the Ribble Ribble just off the A59, is now in ruins, but in its day was a Cistercian Monastery built in 1147 for the Newminster Abbey monks of Northumberland. Legend has it that there is an underground tunnel leading to Whalley Abbey and that monks used to travel through the tunnel between the abbeys for safety. The spirit of a black, hooded monk has often been seen floating around the abbey and on the road outside, as far down as the river and the road bridge which crosses it.

The bridge at Sawley © Craig Bryant

In 1998 the Bolton Evening News reported on a resident of Whalley being terrified by the apparition of a beautiful young girl that appeared in his bedroom for no less than 10 nights on the run! Rumours of the beautiful spirit abound in the village of Whalley and many believe the manifestation to be the ghost of a nun who worked in the Abbey before it was closed in 1536.

Not all the monks in the Abbey were gentlemen and she was believed to have been abused and kept there against her will. Legend has it that she was murdered trying to escape because the monks were afraid she would tell her Mother Superior how she was treated. The body was believed to have been buried in the grounds of the abbey.

There is also a legend of a White Lady which haunts Whalley Abbey, and she has been seen as a white flash in one of the top floor windows. She is believed to be the wife of Ralph Ashton who purchased the abbey from The Crown for £2000 following Henry VIII's dissolution of the Monasteries, and she is believed to have once lived in the house. Loving it so much that when she died, she refused to leave! She is often seen in the winter months in the Great Hall, warming herself by the fire.

Every Lancashire town can boast of ghostly sightings. Accrington, the town where I spent the first 38 years of my life, is famous for a number of well-known hauntings. One of the most famous is that of a ghostly girl who fell in love with a Monk from the (now ruined) Cistercian Abbey situated on Black Abbey Street, near the River Hyndburn. She of course came to a tragic end, and her ghost is occasionally seen floating around the site of the old Abbey, wringing her hands in desperation as she searches for her long-departed love. A row of shops on Warner Street are reputedly haunted, and local Paranormal Groups have catalogued all manner of ghostly activity during their nocturnal vigils.

There are ghostly animals too. Every country lane or secluded hamlet tells of 'Striker', a monstrous ghoulish black dog with eyes as wide as saucers, who foretells of a death in the family of anyone unfortunate enough to encounter it. There is even a ghostly rabbit from Rochdale! The Baum Rabbit is rather famous in those parts, and is still talked about in whispers by the older generation who recall that saying its name out loud often brought bad luck.

Ghostly 'Hell Hounds' are famous throughout the British Isles, and Manchester has its very own 'Black Shuck'. This grisly apparition can appear headless, or with huge burning red eyes and is a harbinger of ill fortune and death. Legend says that it was laid to rest under a bridge over the River Irwell after if terrified local folk around the cathedral for years. In Lancashire, this black hound is called Barguist, Grim, Gytrash, Padfoot, Shag, Skriker or Striker, and Trash. In Lytham, on the Ribble Estuary, 'Skriker' haunts the salt marshes, often seen when the mist descends on calm, moonless nights.

The Fylde Coast boasts numerous other hauntings, including the spectral lady of Lytham Hall. There are ghostly ships gliding silently up the Ribble Estuary on foggy, moonless nights with a hold full of contraband, heading for the creeks of Freckleton and Warton Bank. Even more disturbing are 'Wreckers', phantom lights that mimic lighthouses, luring ships to crash against the shore on stormy nights.

The Ship Inn at Freckleton was once a famous haunt of smugglers and pirates and this venerable old pub has many stories of ghosts and strange happenings. It was, for a long time, home to a human skull which resided in the attic. In the mid 1990's the owners of the pub realised it had gone, and suddenly manifestations started happening. One of the waitresses saw two people sat in the dining area dressed in 'red shirts and white bloomers' deep in conversation. As the pub was closed, she went to get the manager, thinking they were diners who had not finished their meals, and that they must be taking part in some sort of fancy dress or hunt and been unwittingly locked in. When he went into the dining room to ask them to politely leave, they were gone. Interestingly, as the pub was closed all the entrances were locked and there was no way they could have got out. The skull has never been seen since. A cottage close to The Ship Inn also has its resident ghost, that of a 'river raider'. These were men who used to watch for merchant ships travelling up the Ribble channel from the Ship Inn and signal their cohorts when one was spotted. They would then raid the boat and steal its valuable cargo. By all accounts, the ghost can be very unpleasant and make you feel uncomfortable if he does not like you, but can also make you feel comfortable if he does.

The Ship and Royal Hotel on Clifton Street in Lytham has had many reports of a male manifestation that hovers around the bar and disturbs paperwork. He has been known to even play around with the telephone!

And finally, there are Fairies. Many legends of the tiny folk and 'Fairy Circles', small circles of grassy tussocks found in unploughed fields, abound in Lancashire. From the Fairly Steps of Silverdale to the nocturnal sightings in Cat Bells Wood near Grindleton in the Ribble Valley, sightings of these magical and elusive little people are rare, but not entirely undocumented by those 'in the know'. However, the author can say with much certainty, that whilst he may have seen many strange things in Lancashire in his time, Fairies were not one of them!

Printed in Great Britain
by Amazon